Wishing you all the best !
Harpinder.

All The Very Best
Lynda Hughes

Lana,
May you have love, success
and good health in the future.
all our best,
Leslie

Good Luck
Frank Case

God's love has always been
our lives foundation.
Wishing you the best.
Rebecca Joe

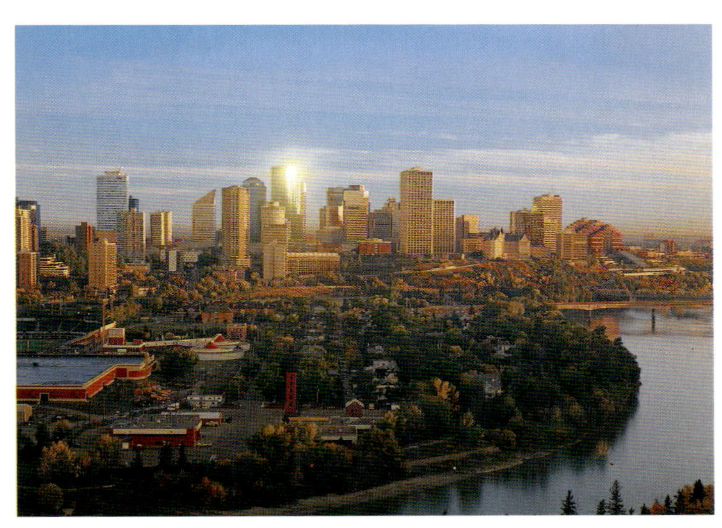

EDMONTON

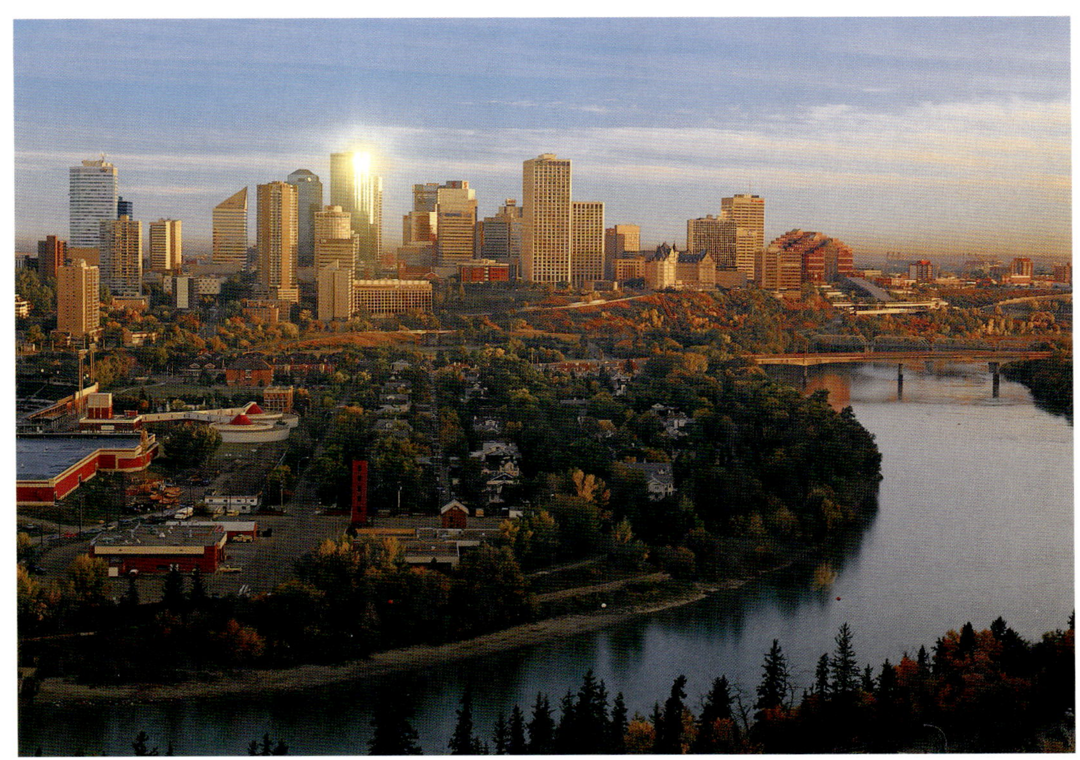

WHITECAP BOOKS
VANCOUVER / TORONTO / NEW YORK

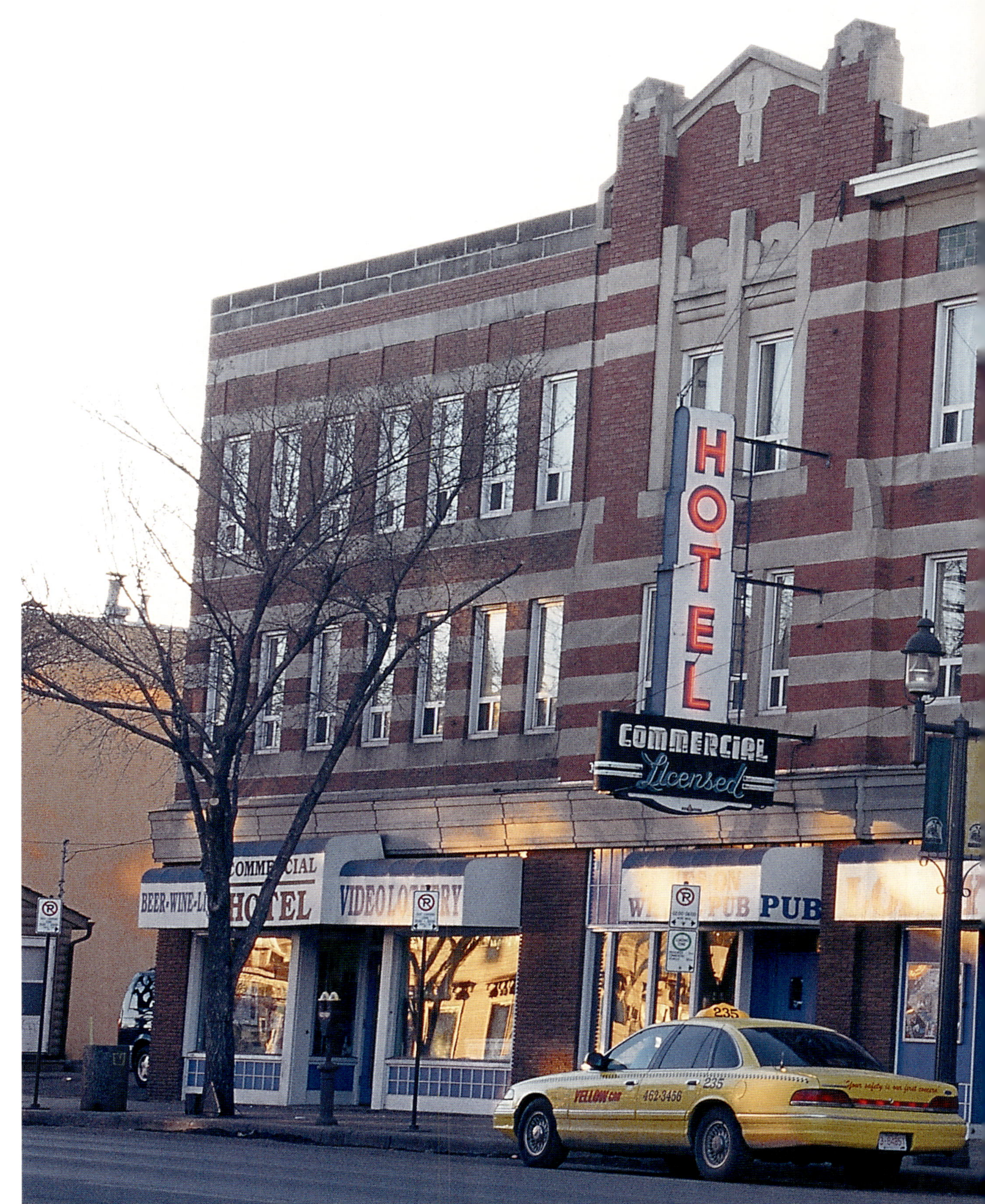

Visitors in Old Strathcona wander from café to coffee shop, antique market to vintage clothing store. Eight theatres and the annual Fringe Festival make this a favourite cultural destination, while the restored storefronts and offices along Whyte Avenue entice history buffs.

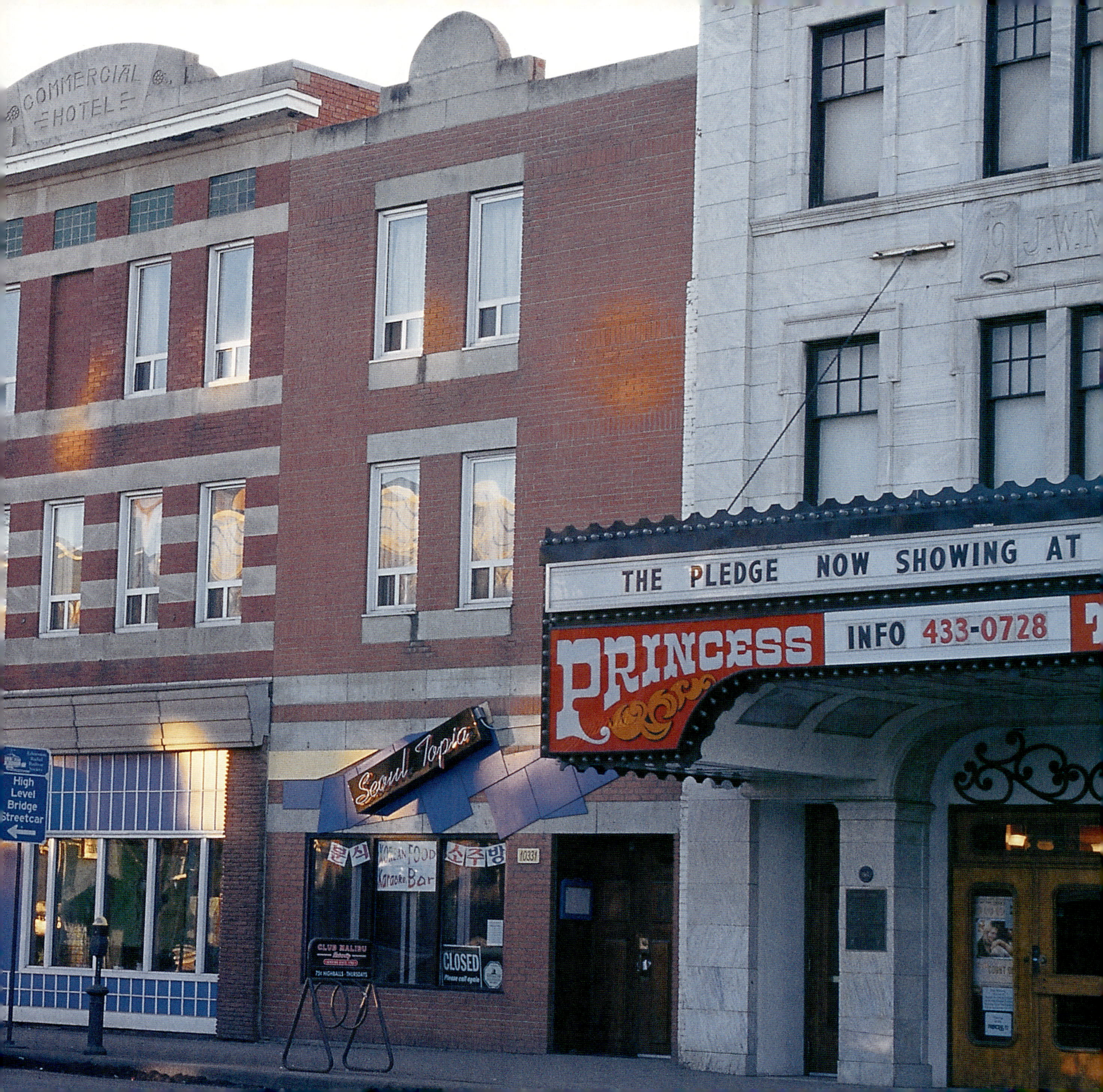
COMMERCIAL HOTEL
High Level Bridge Streetcar
Seoul Topia
분식
KOREAN FOOD Karaoke Bar
소주방
10331
CLUB MALIBU
75¢ HIGHBALLS - THURSDAYS
CLOSED
Please call again
THE PLEDGE NOW SHOWING AT
PRINCESS
INFO 433-0728

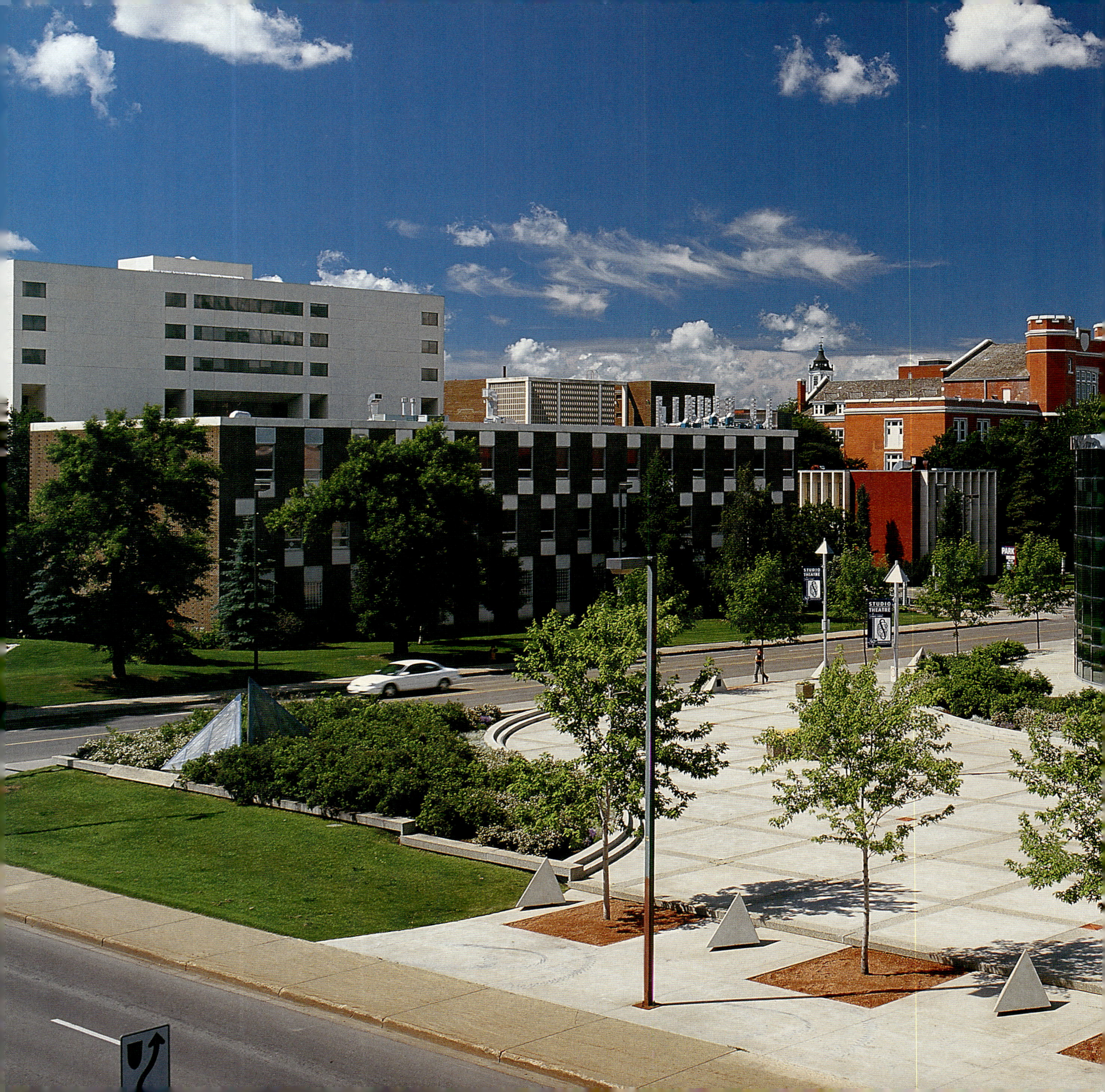

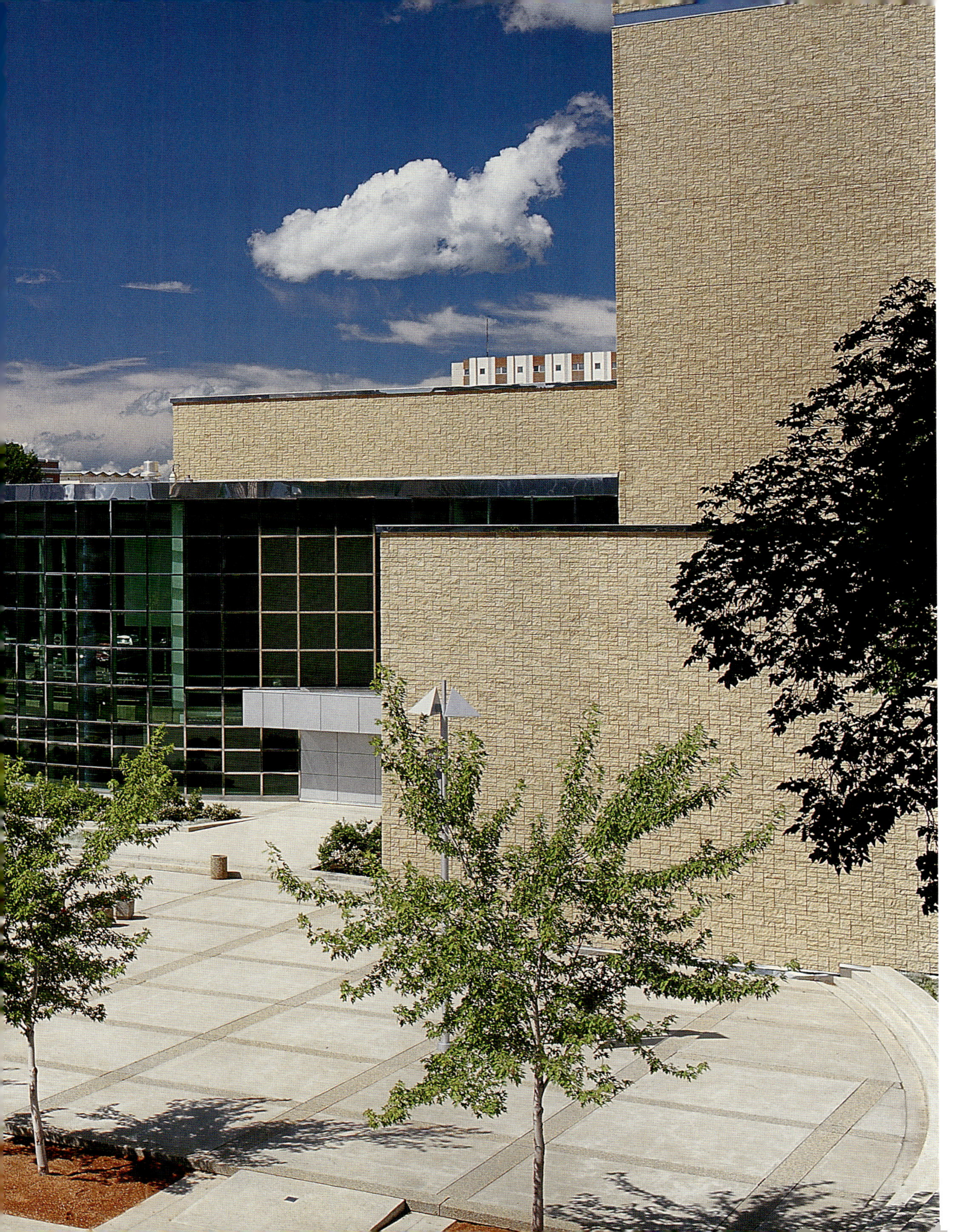

The province's largest research centre and post-secondary school, the University of Alberta caters to 30,000 students and offers more than 350 graduate and undergraduate programs.

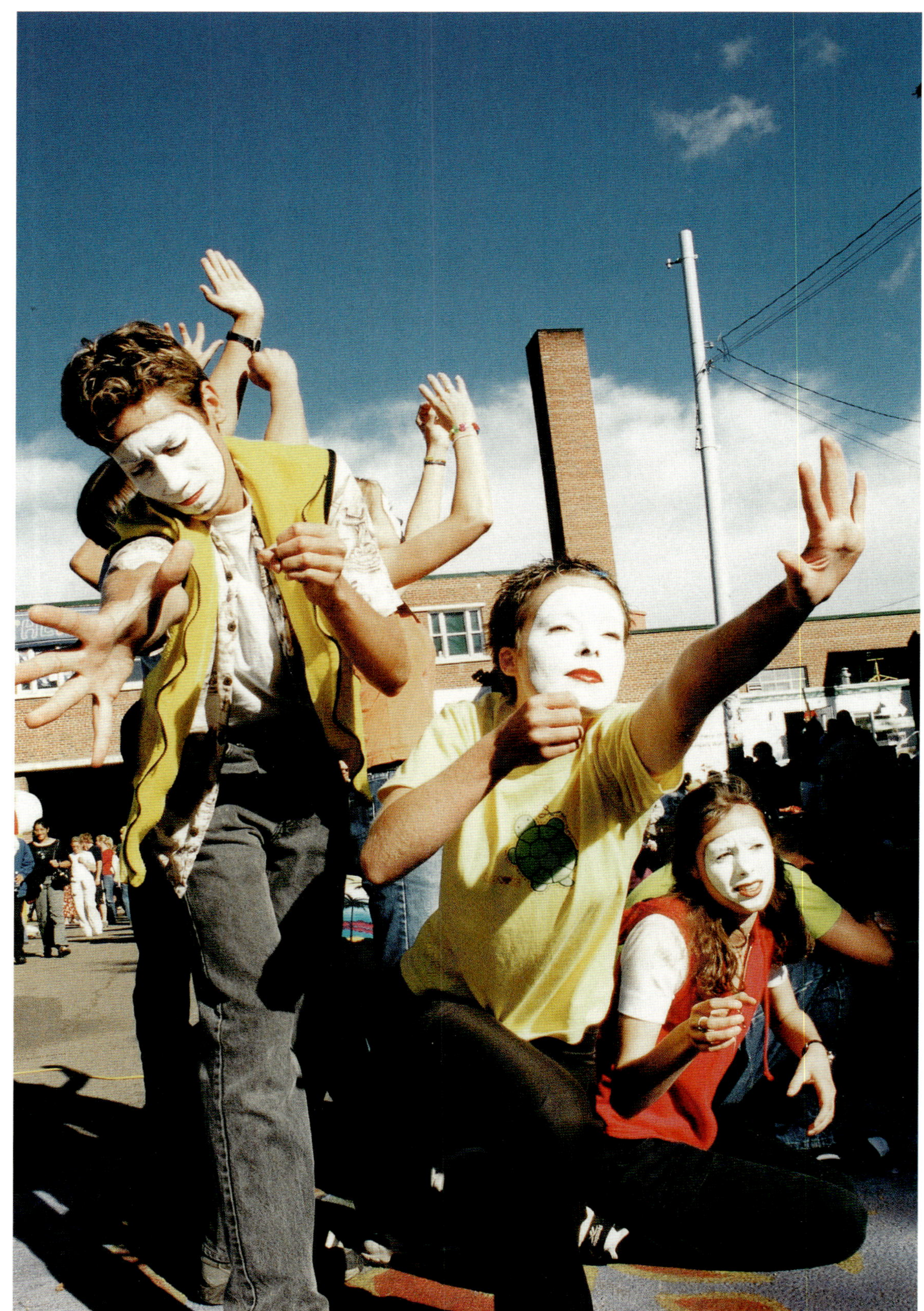

Edmonton's Fringe Festival brings more than 400,000 people to Old Strathcona each year for the nation's oldest and largest fringe. Young playwrights showcase their best works in the neighbourhood's theatres, while other entertainment beckons the crowds outside.

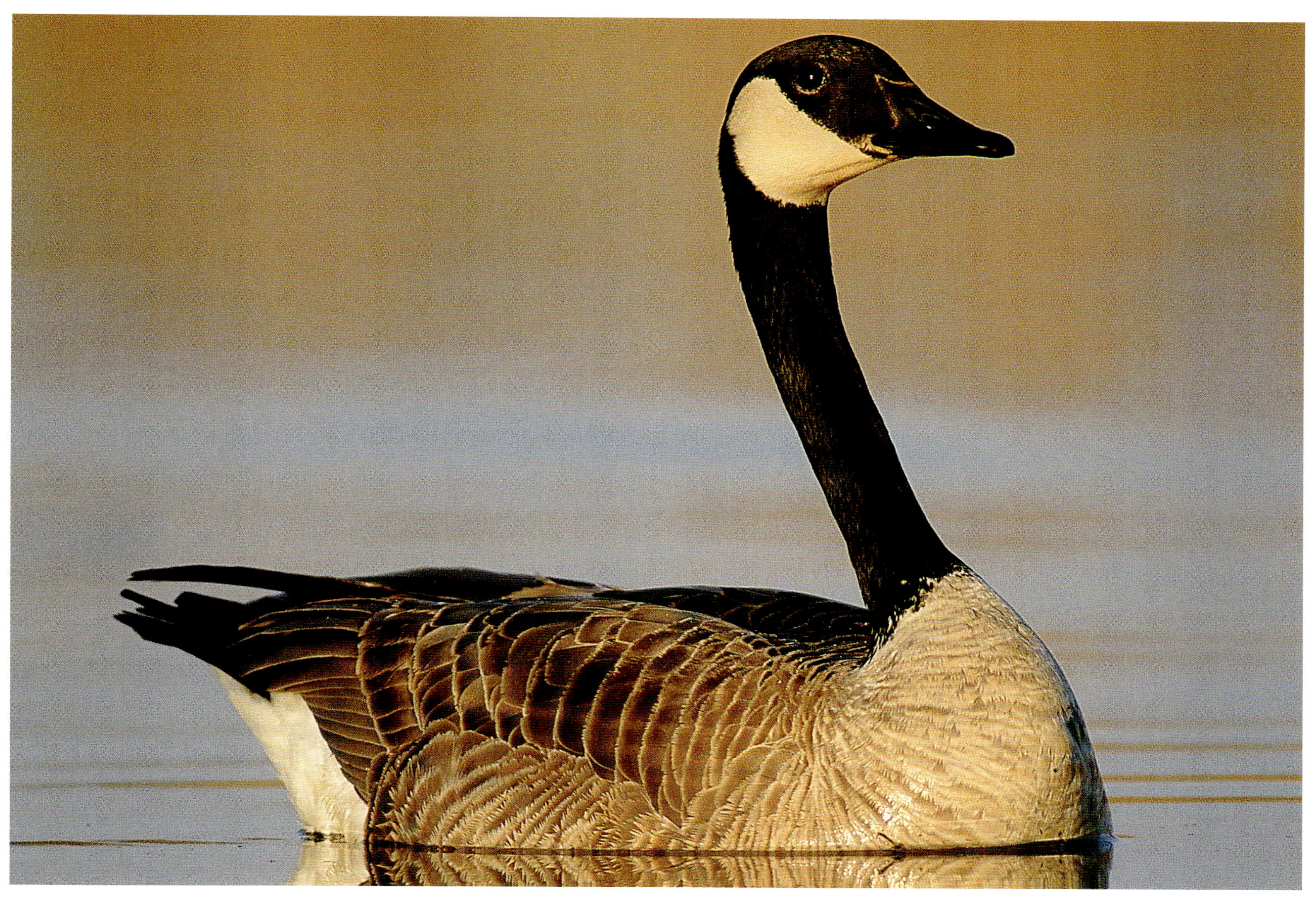

Edmonton has more green space than any other city in Canada. A favourite picnic spot for residents and University of Alberta students is Emily Murphy Park on the North Saskatchewan River's south bank.

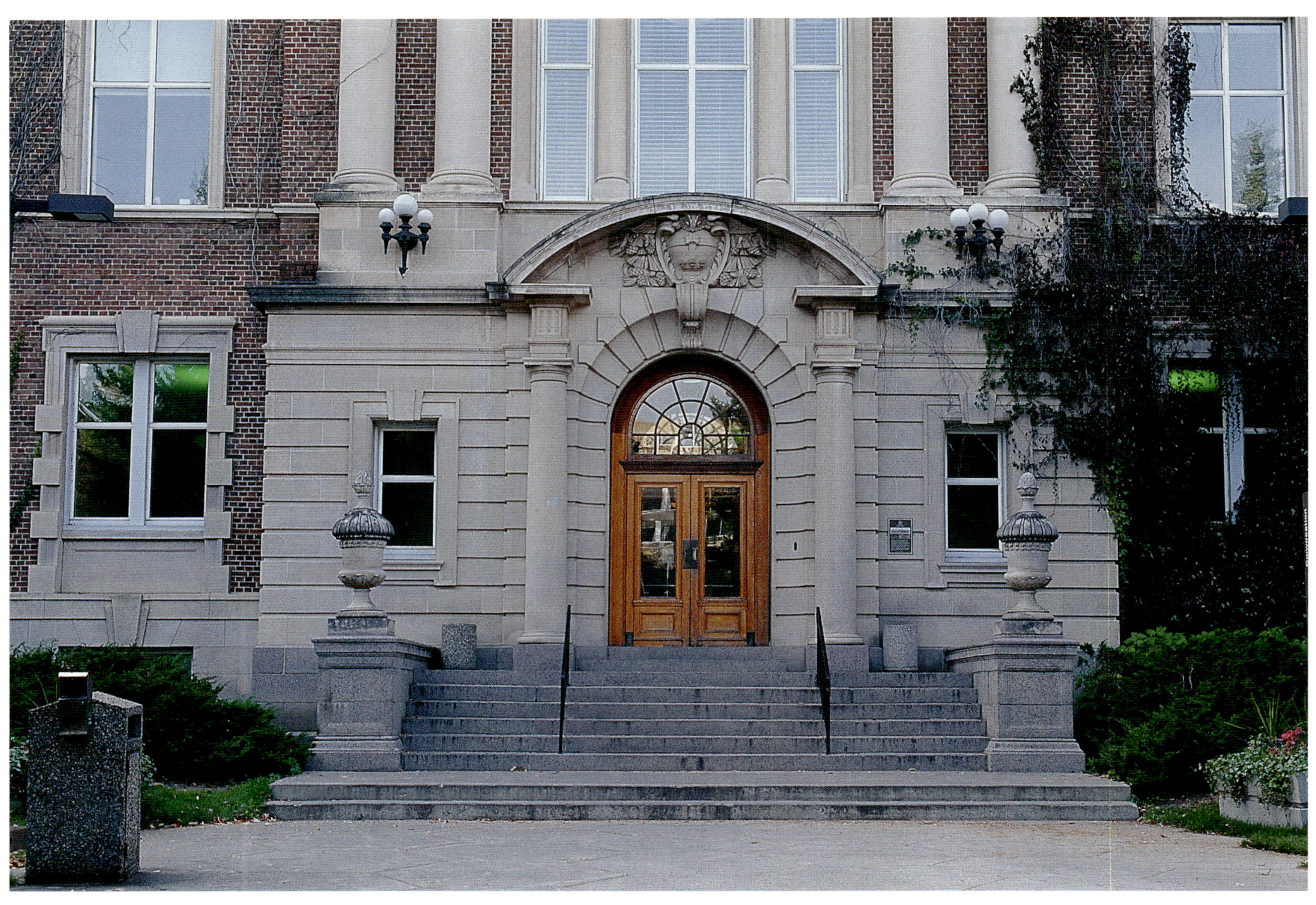

Within the university's 89 hectares (2,200 acres) there are 90 buildings, more than 400 laboratories, and the second-largest research library in the nation, housing 5.3 million books.

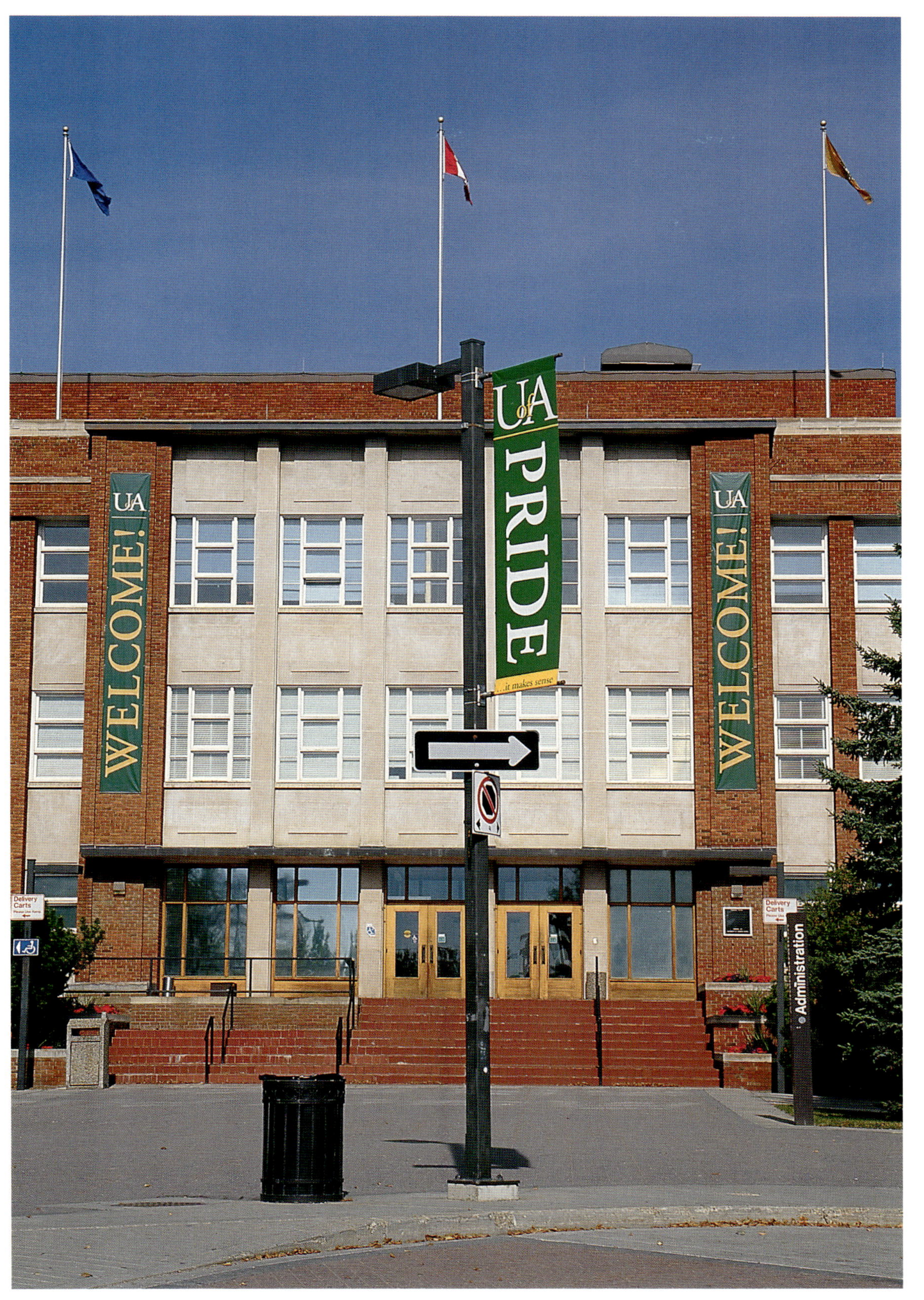

The University of Alberta's distinguished alumni include former prime minister Joe Clark, Supreme Court Chief Justice Beverly McLachlin, and former governor general Roland Michener, along with prize-winning novelists, athletes, and scientists.

Jubilee Auditorium seats 2,750 people for concerts, musicals, university events and more. Queen Elizabeth and Prince Philip attended Commonwealth Games events here in 1978 and the University of Alberta later awarded Prince Charles an honorary degree during his visit with Lady Diana.

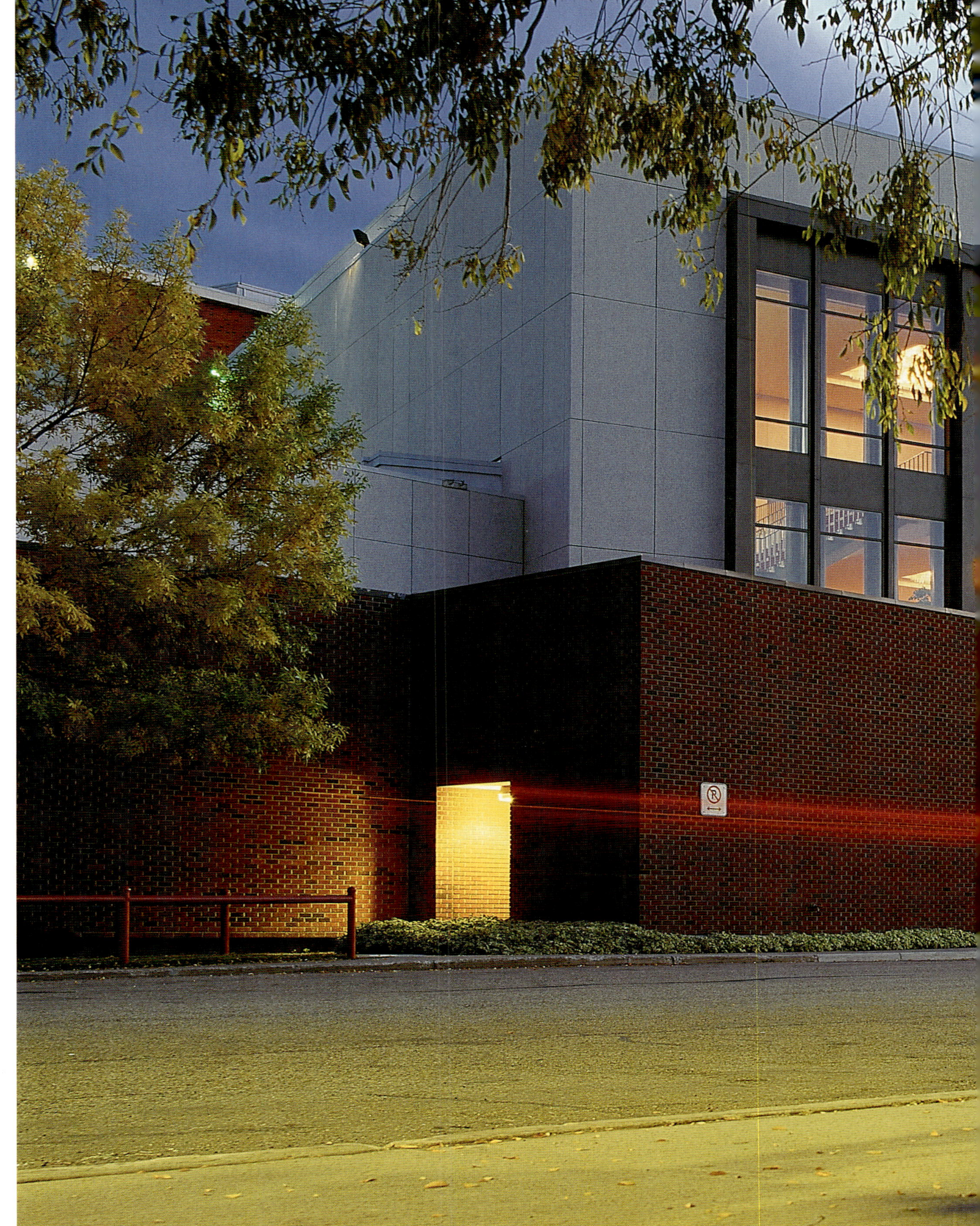

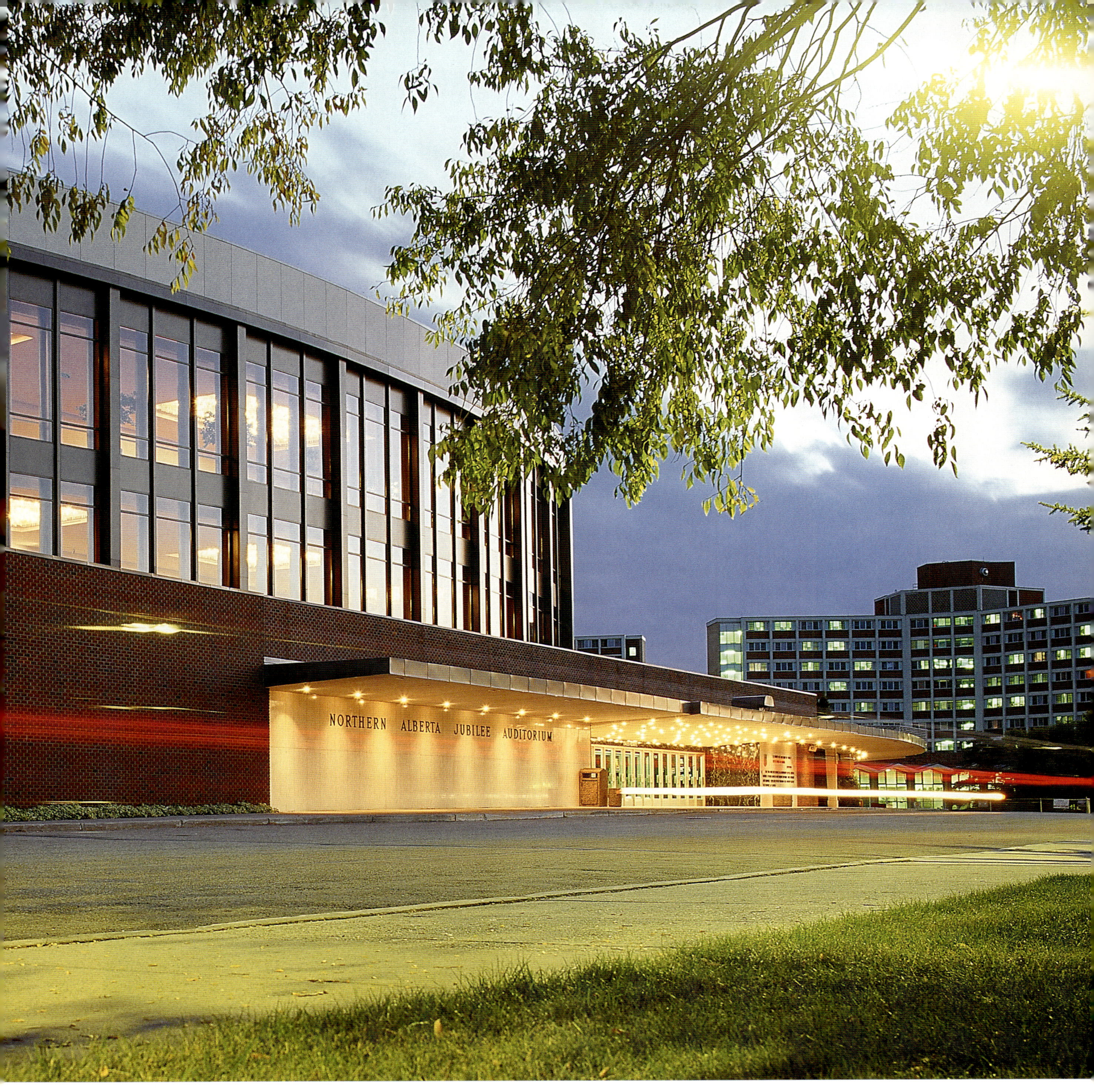
NORTHERN ALBERTA JUBILEE AUDITORIUM

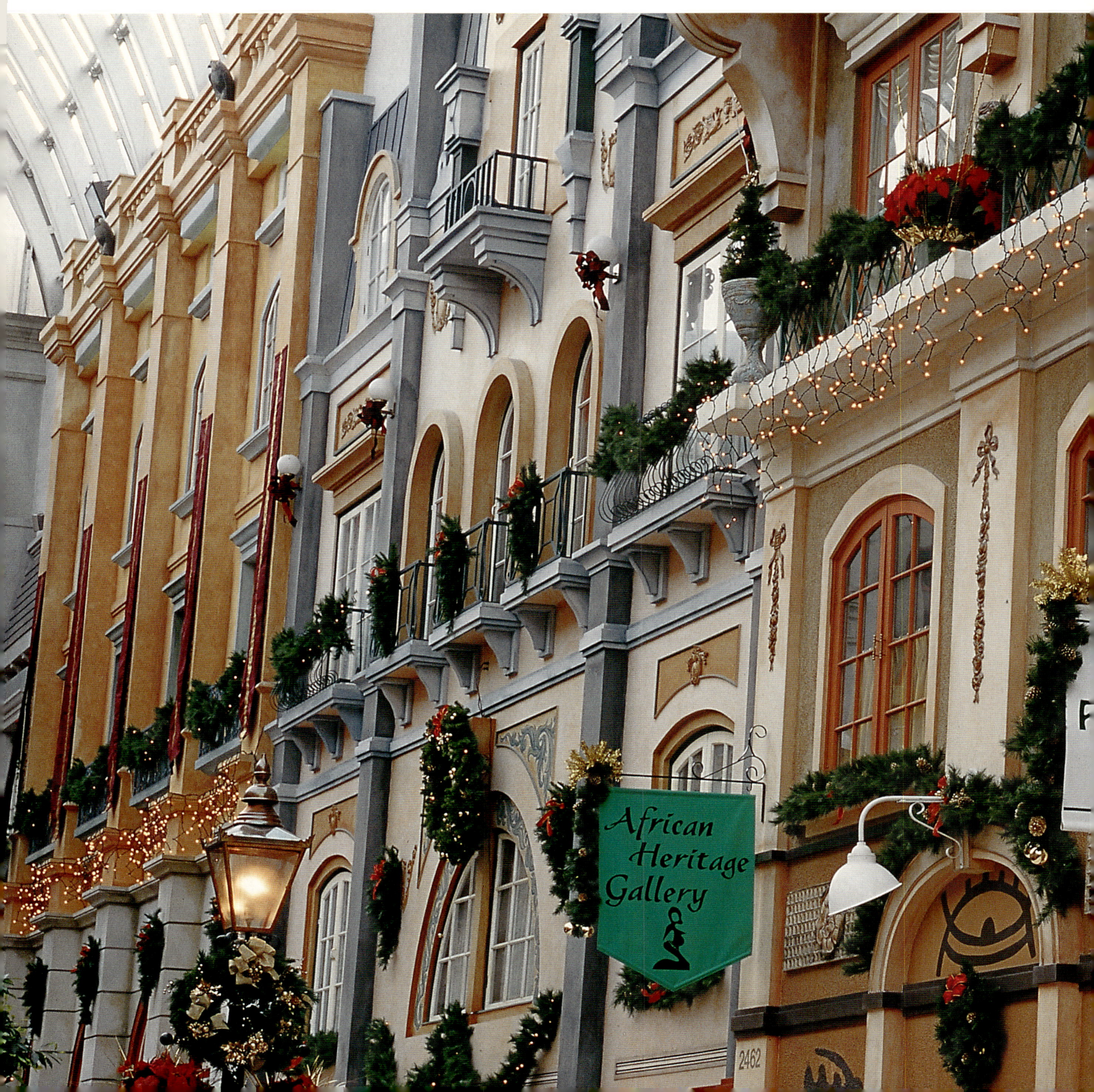
African
Heritage
Gallery
2462

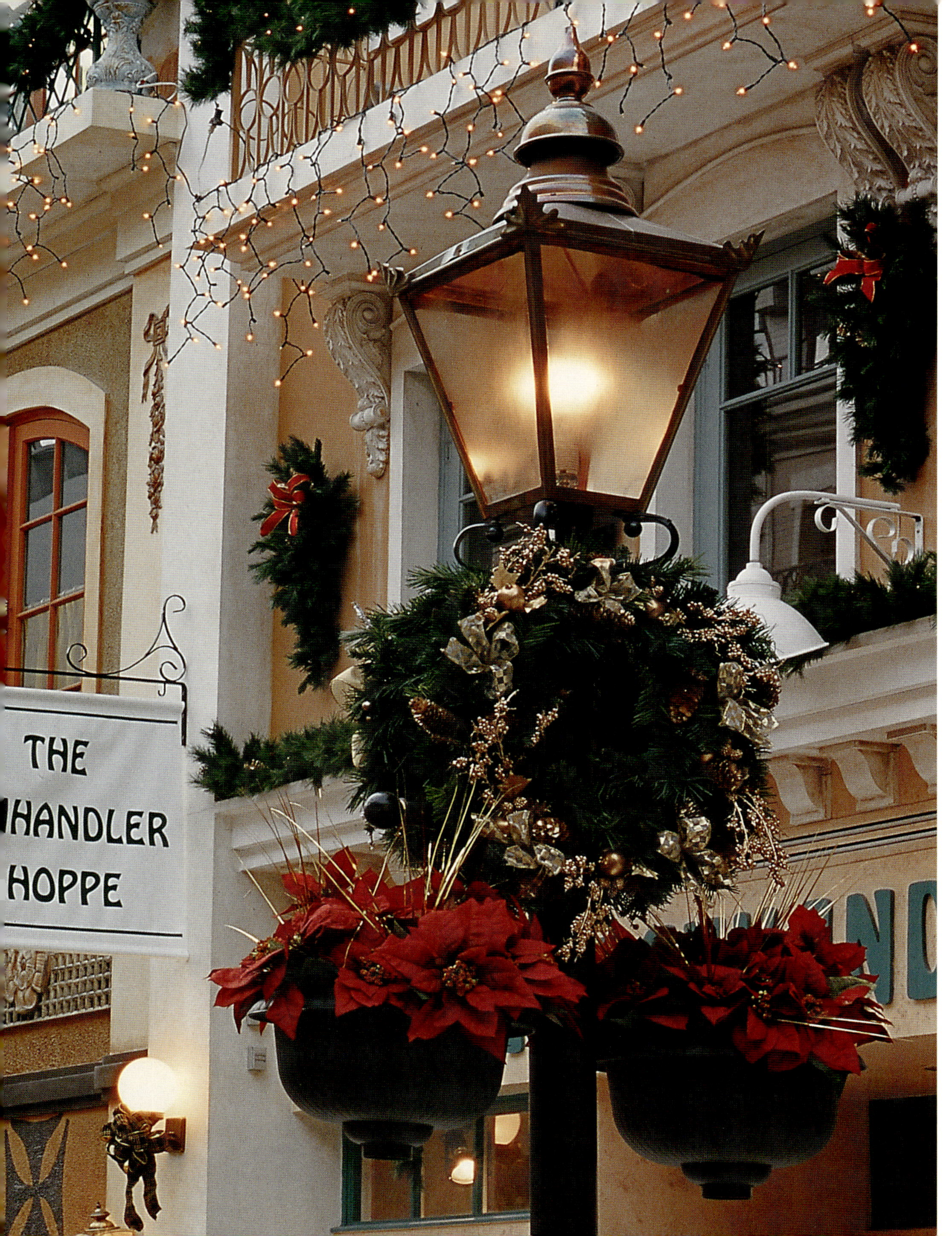

Europa Boulevard in West Edmonton Mall brings the world to Edmonton's doorstep. European-style bistros spill into the "street," offering international flavours to the 20 million visitors who tour this mall each year.

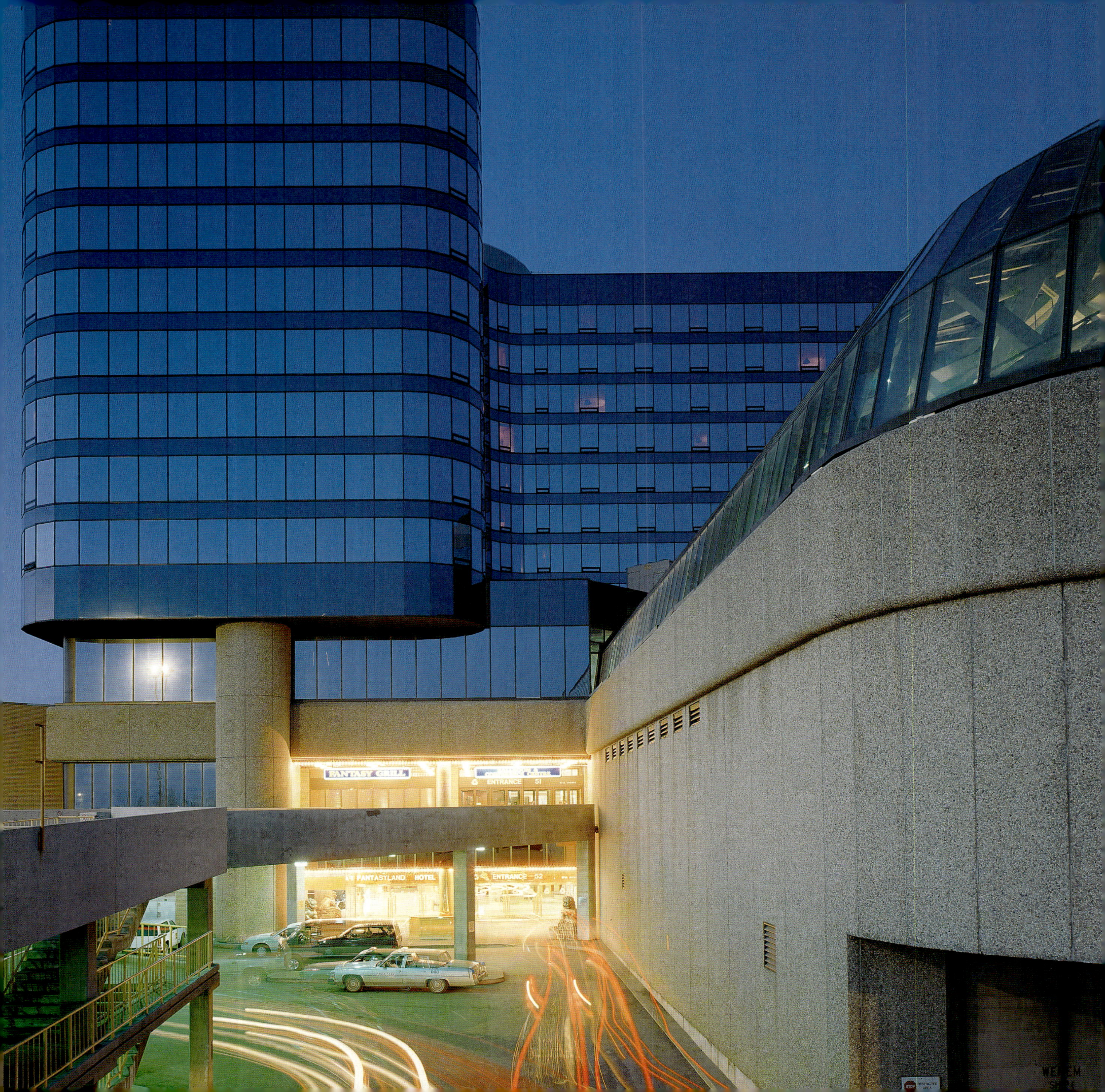
FANTASY GRILL
ENTRANCE 51
FANTASYLAND HOTEL
ENTRANCE 52

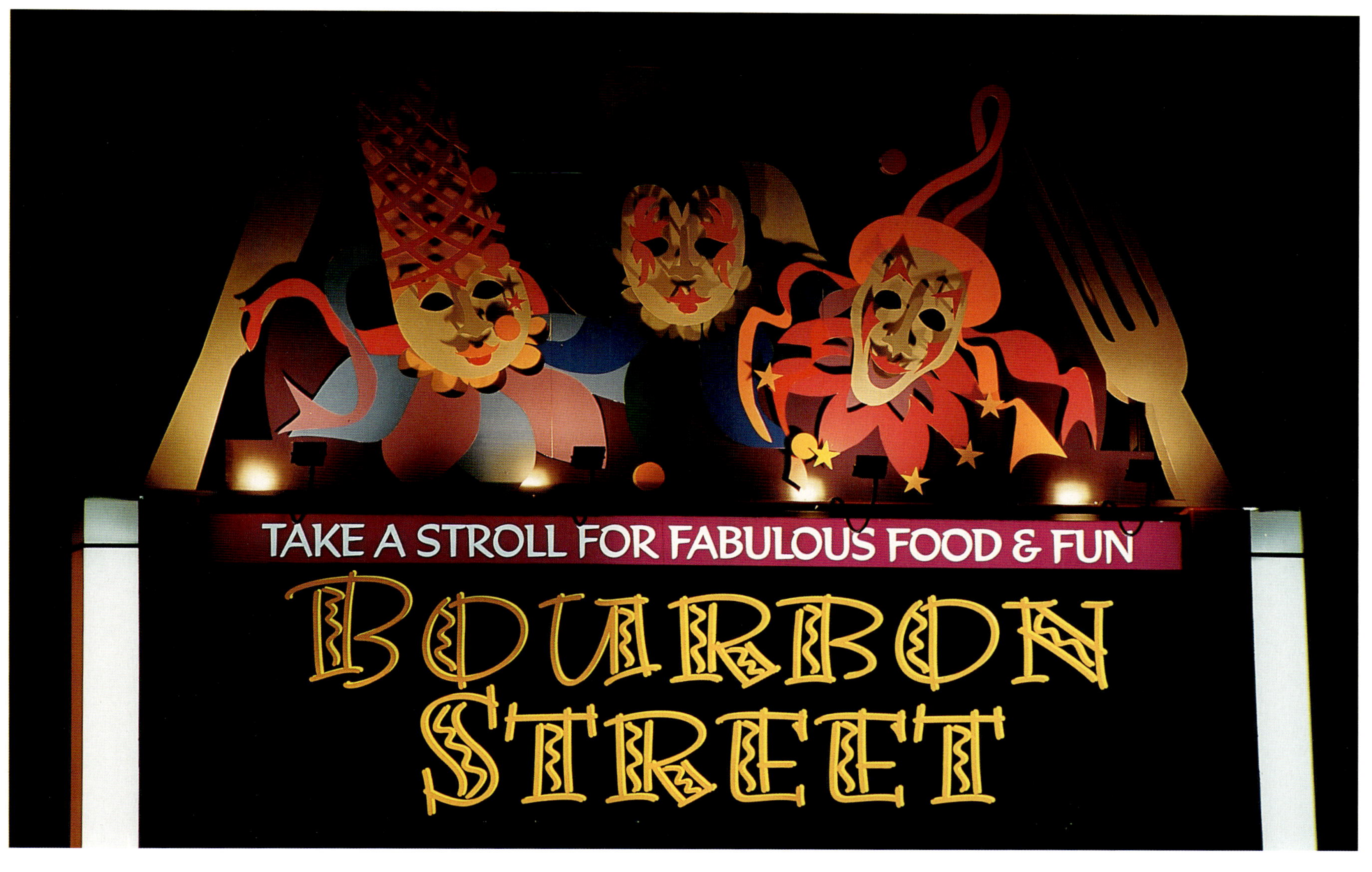

West Edmonton Mall, the largest shopping complex in the world, boasts more than 800 stores in a 48-hectare (119-acre) site. Amusement park rides, submarine tours, the world's largest wave pool, and countless other attractions offer days of entertainment.

Theme rooms at the Fantasyland Hotel transport guests to an Arabian oasis, a jungle safari, an Arctic igloo, or a Polynesian island. Just outside are the myriad stores and restaurants of West Edmonton Mall.

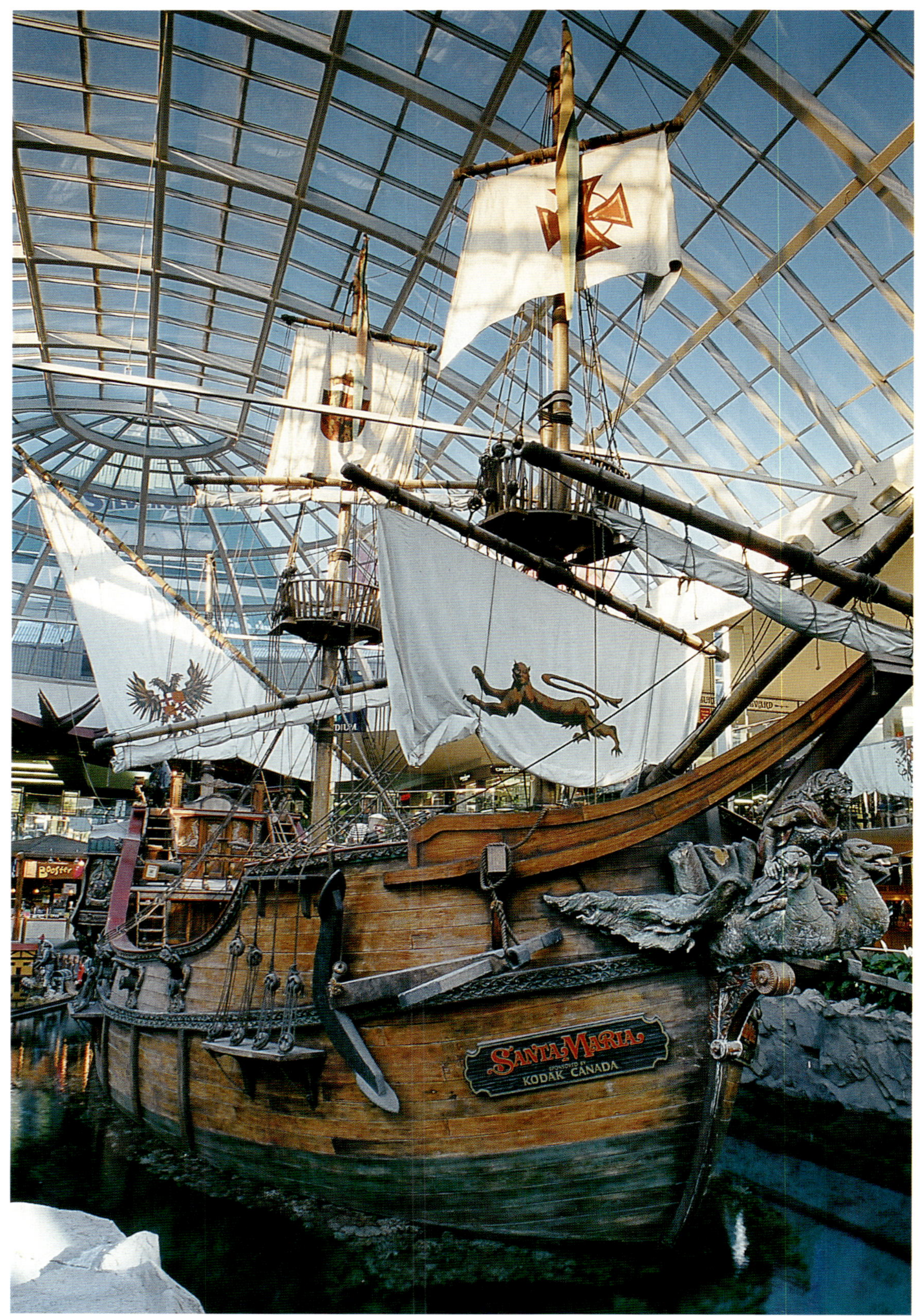

What better ship for the world's largest indoor lake than the *Santa Maria*? This replica of Columbus's famous vessel floats alongside the docks where four working submarines offer underwater adventure.

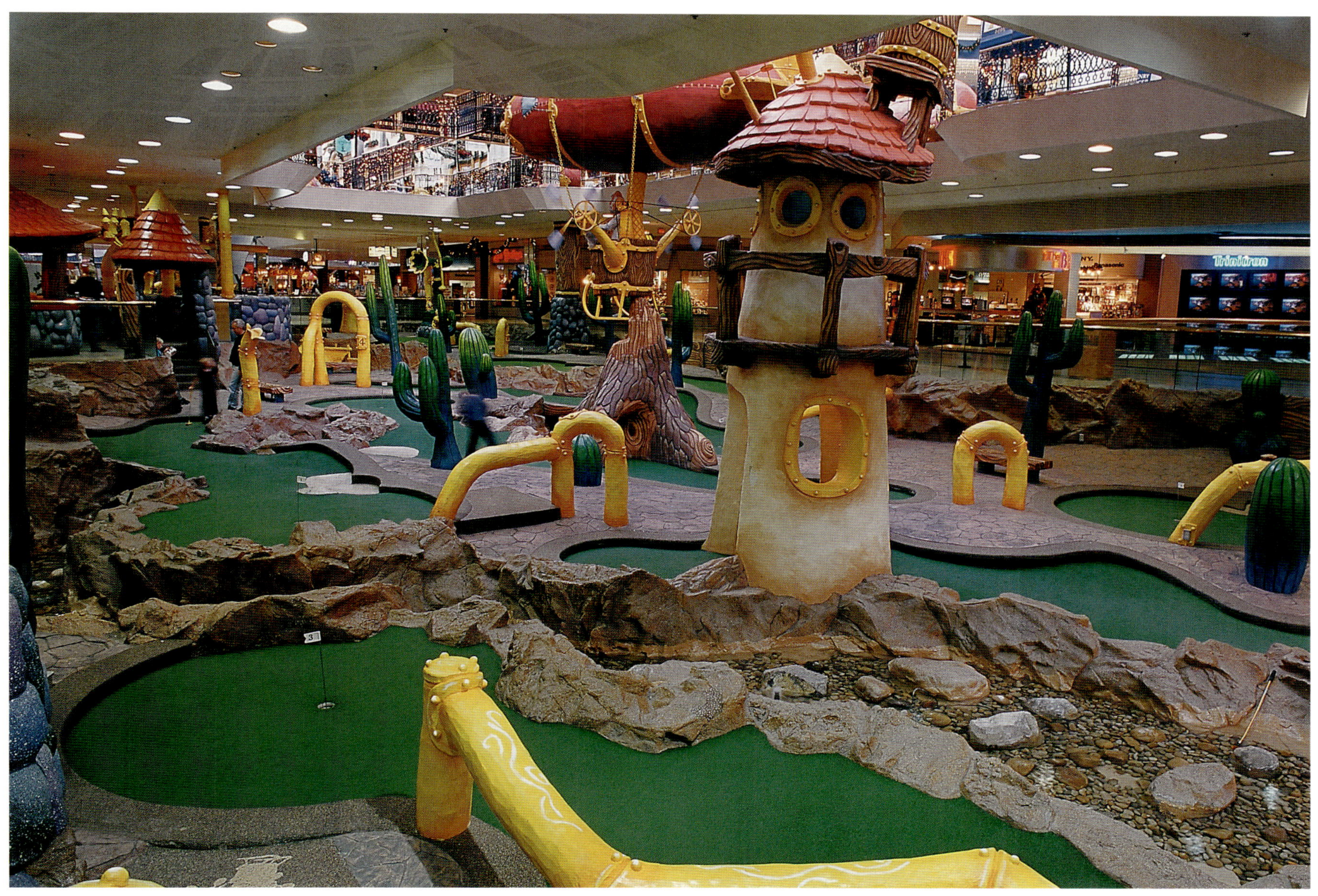

Whimsical cartoon characters draw children and adults into Professor Wem's Adventure Golf. The 18-hole miniature course within West Edmonton Mall is a favourite venue for birthday parties.

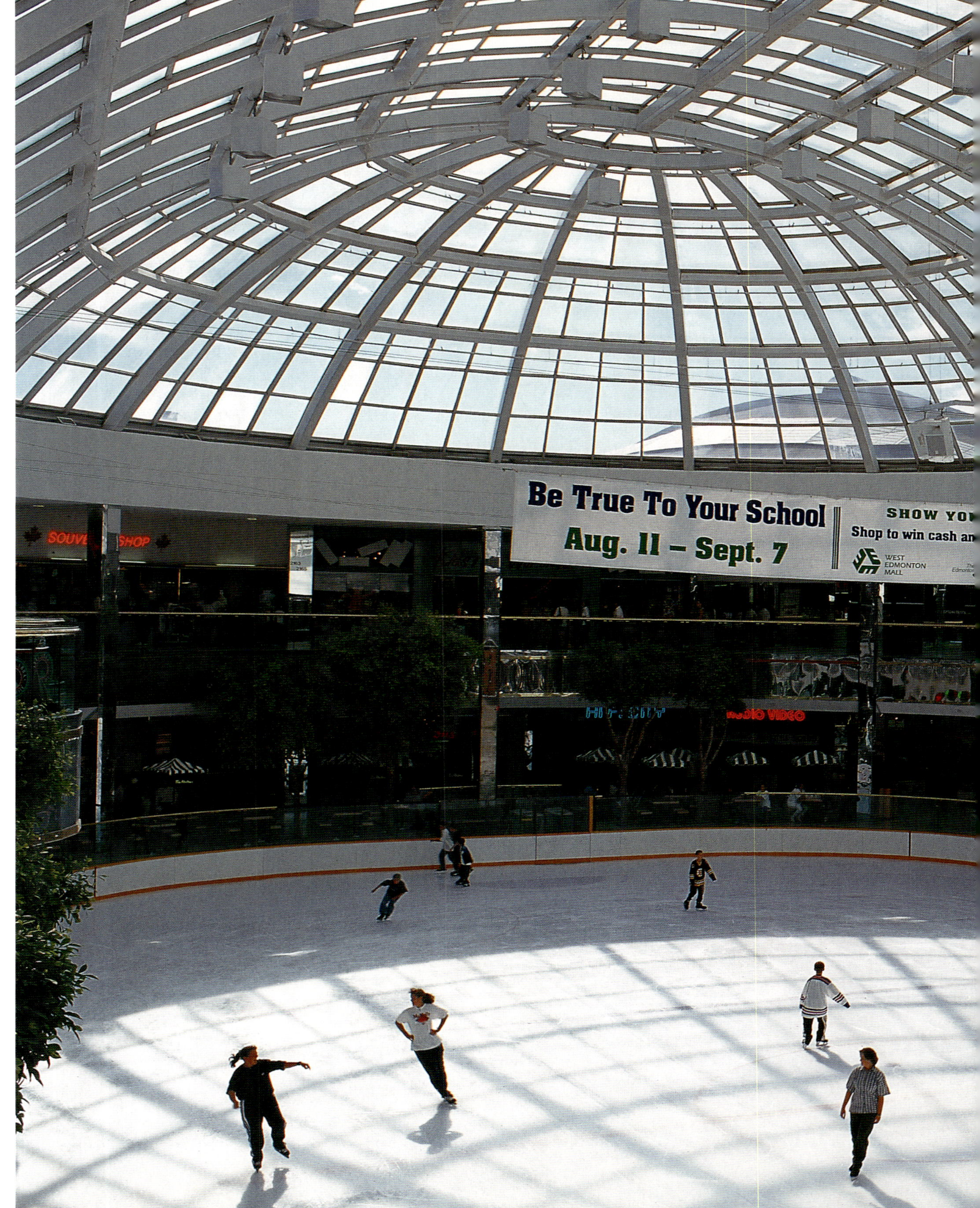

Open year-round, West Edmonton Mall's Ice Palace hosts events ranging from public skating and seniors' programs to Edmonton Oilers hockey practices and figure-skating performances.

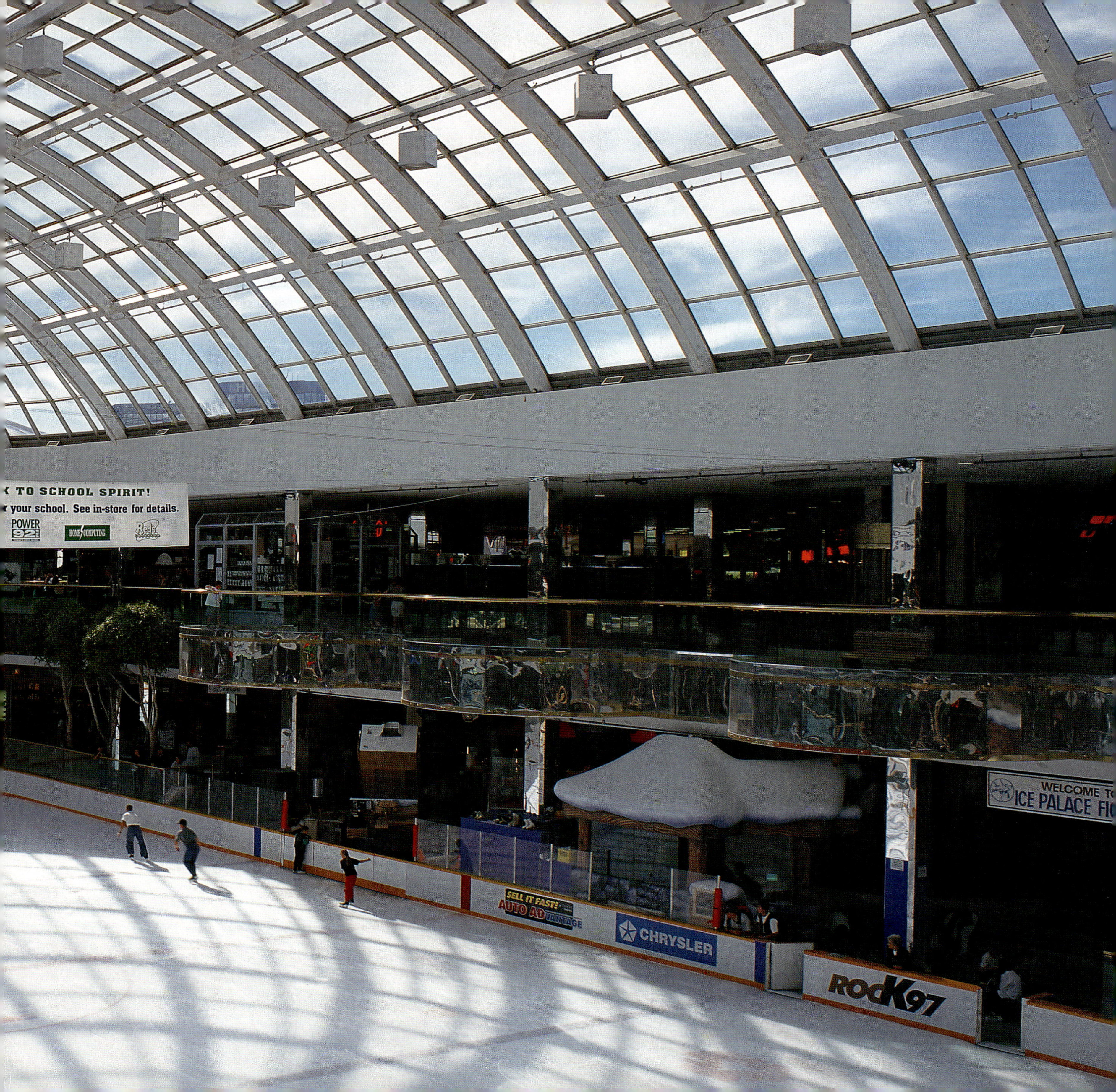
K TO SCHOOL SPIRIT!
r your school. See in-store for details.
POWER 92
HOME COMPUTING
WELCOME TO
ICE PALACE FO
SELL IT FAST!
AUTO ADVANTAGE
CHRYSLER
ROCK97

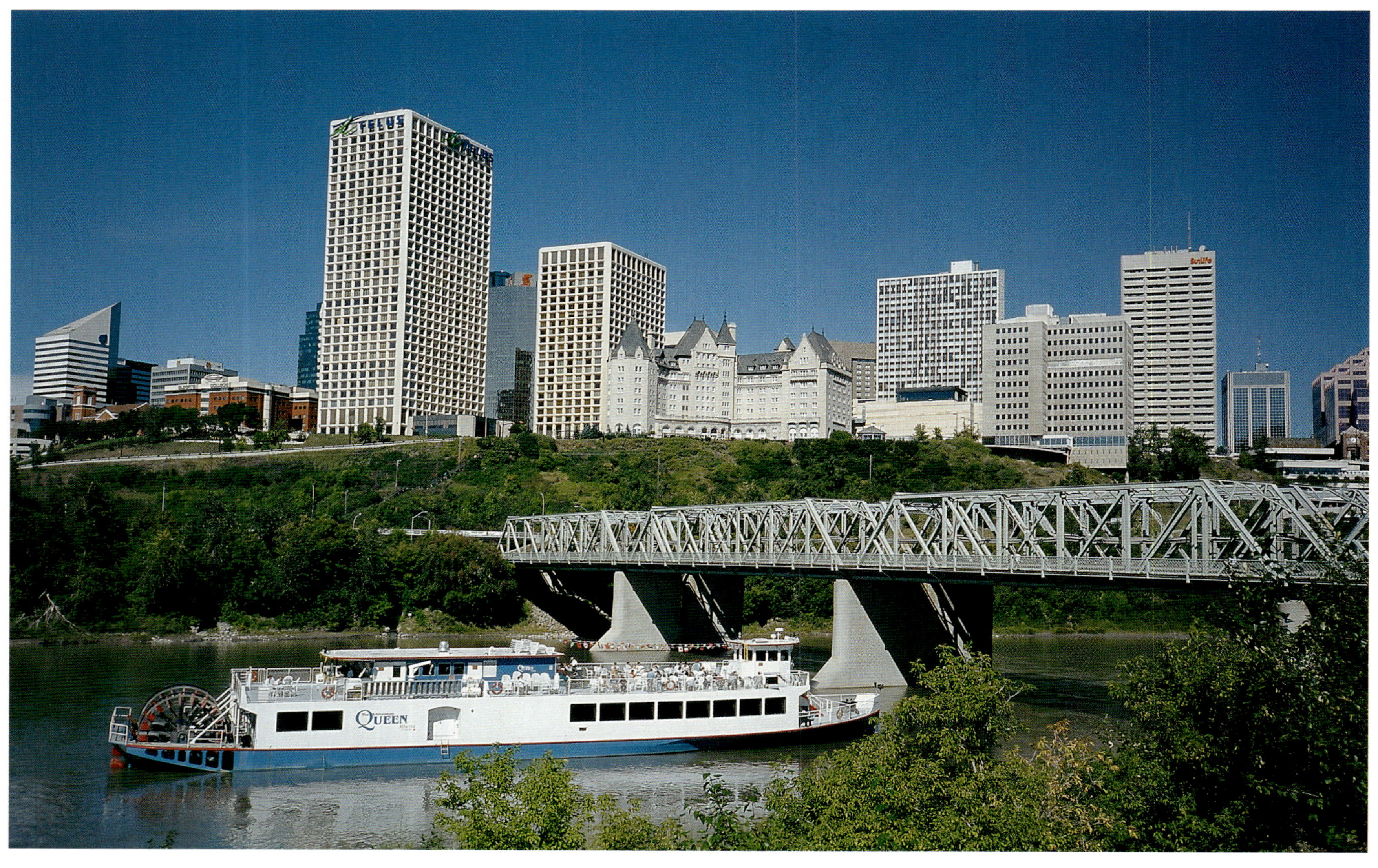

The North Saskatchewan River is born at the base of the Saskatchewan Glacier in the Rockies. Winding through Alberta towards Prince Albert, where it joins the South Saskatchewan River, it eventually flows through Manitoba and into the Nelson River and Hudson Bay.

Traffic pours through the outskirts of the city on Whitemud Drive. Edmonton experienced its largest population boom after 1947, when Alberta's first oil well gushed "black gold." By 1965, there were 10,000 wells bringing new residents and prosperity to the province.

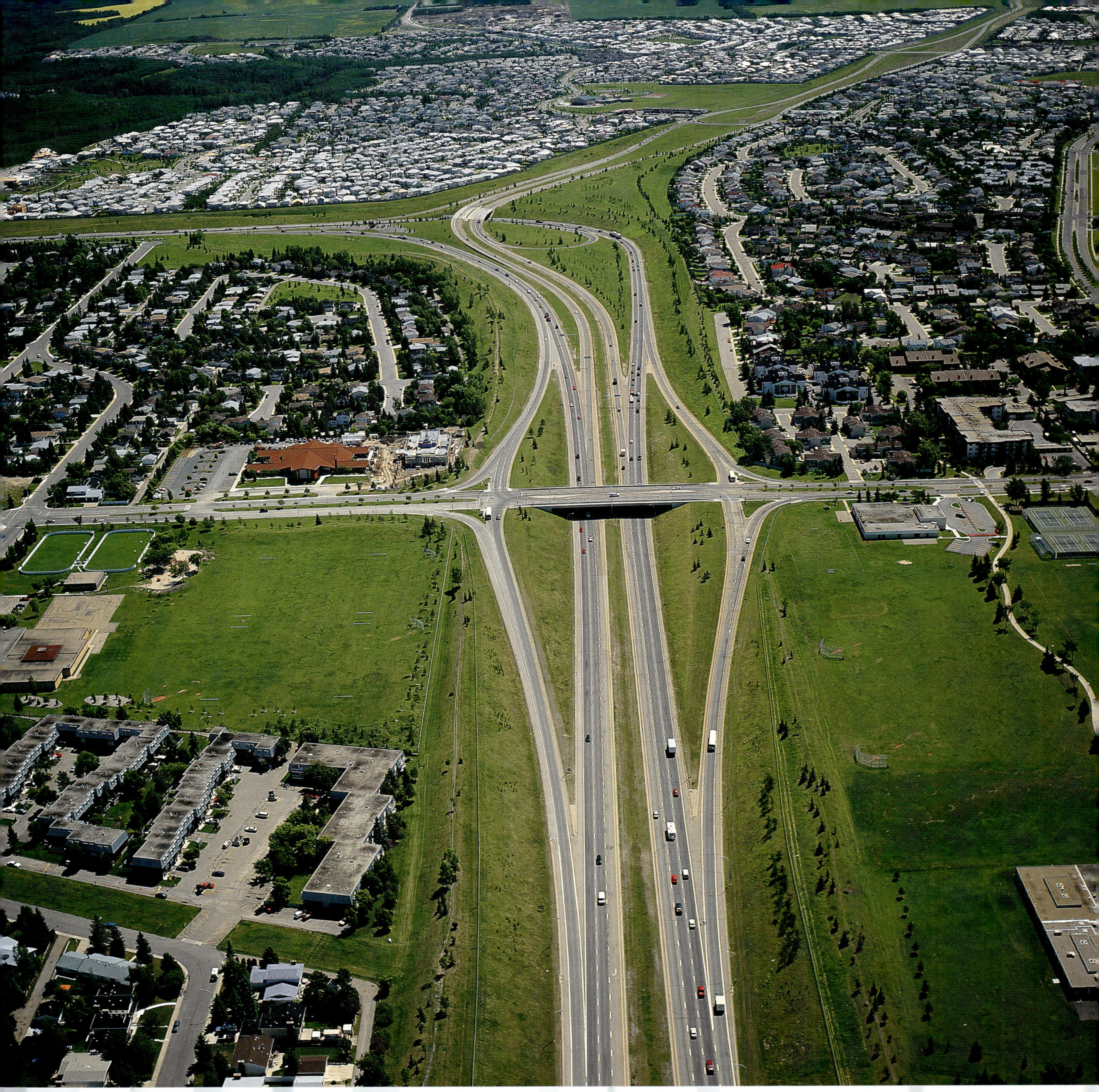

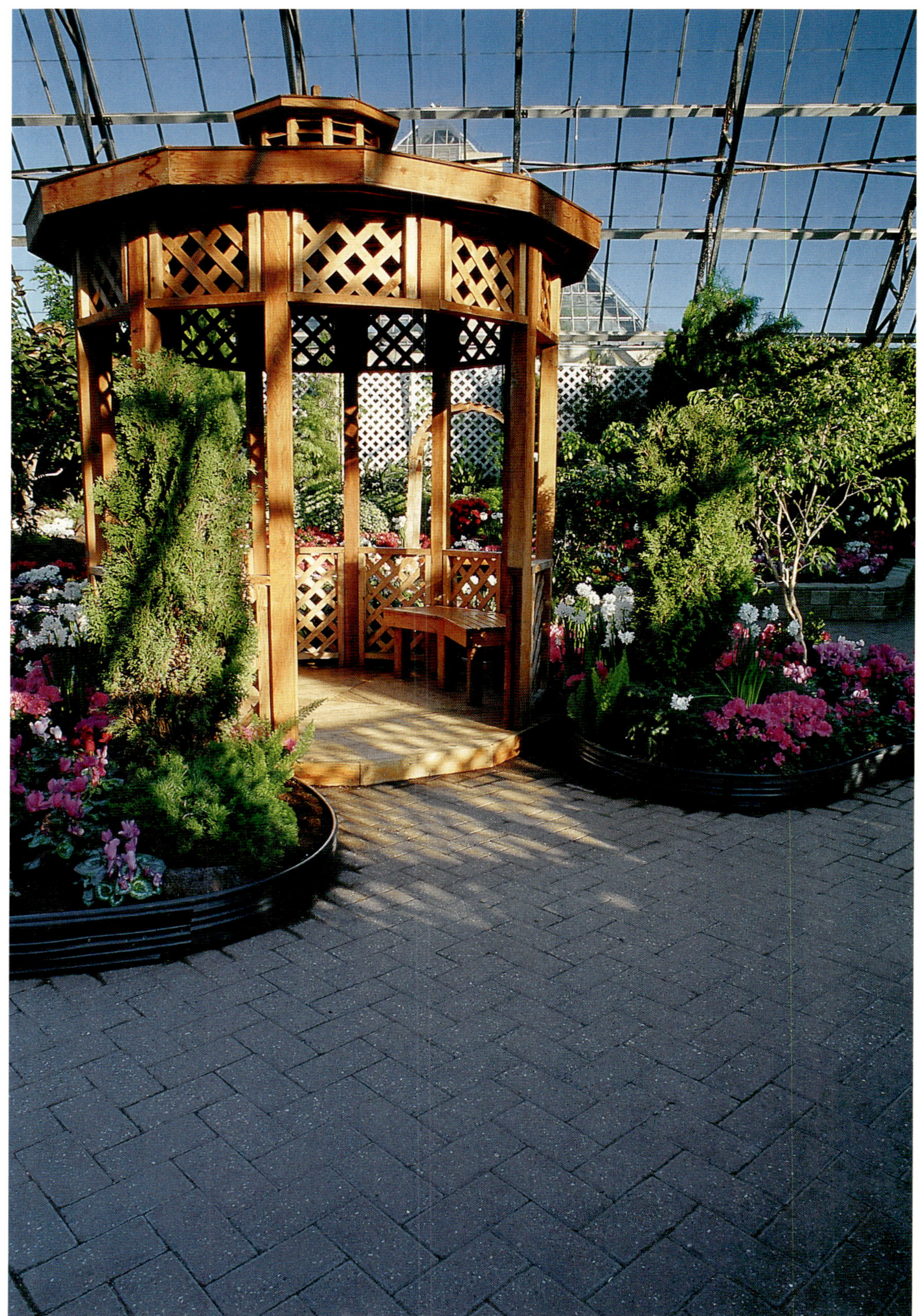

As well as the pyramid pavilions, the conservatory offers new shows and displays with every season. From the orchid show in February to the bonsai exhibit each fall, there is something to attract every green thumb.

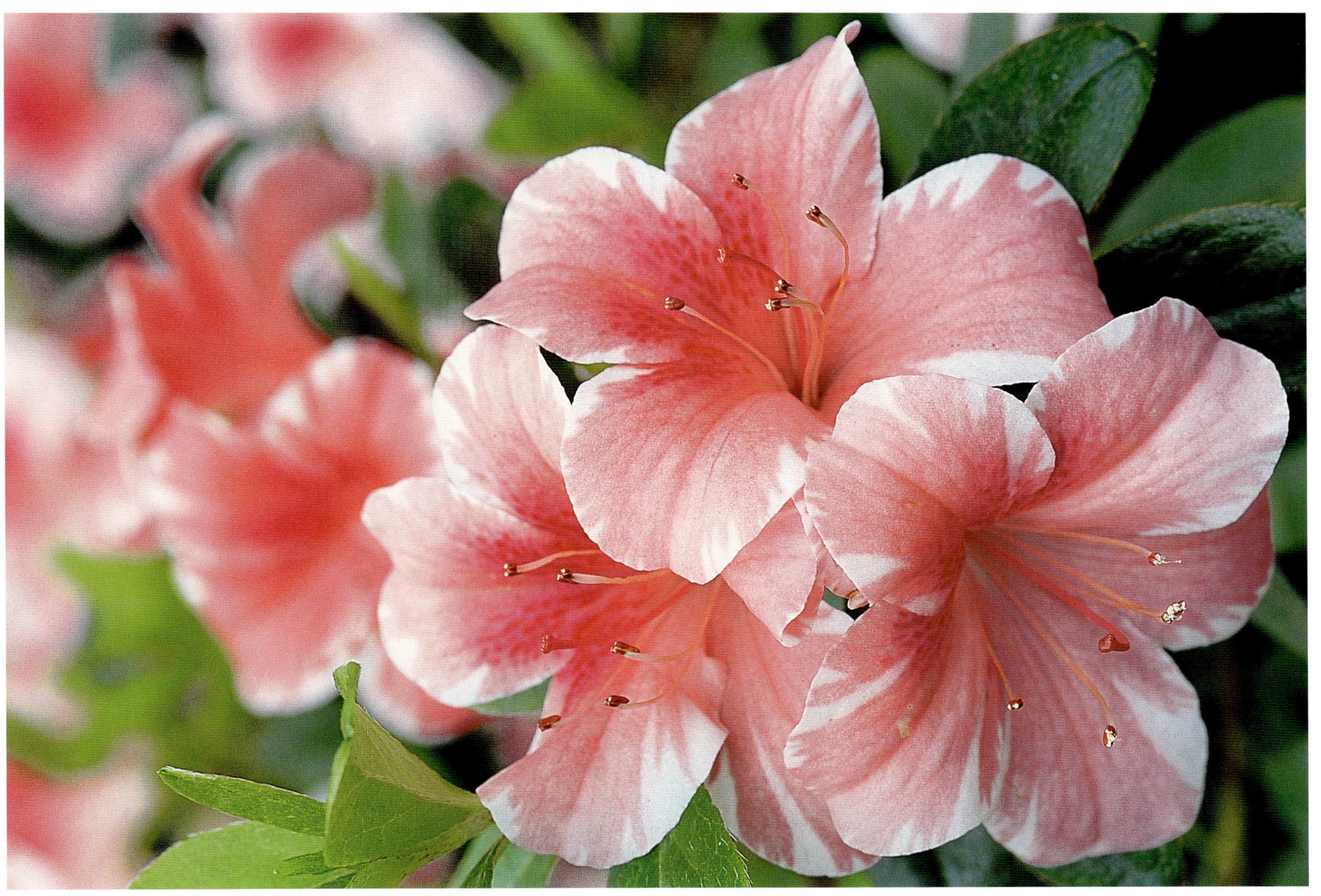

The Muttart Conservatory is as natural an environment as possible — biological pest-control measures include a number of quail that take care of any slugs they come across. Temperatures within the pavilions are adjusted to match the seasons of the original climates.

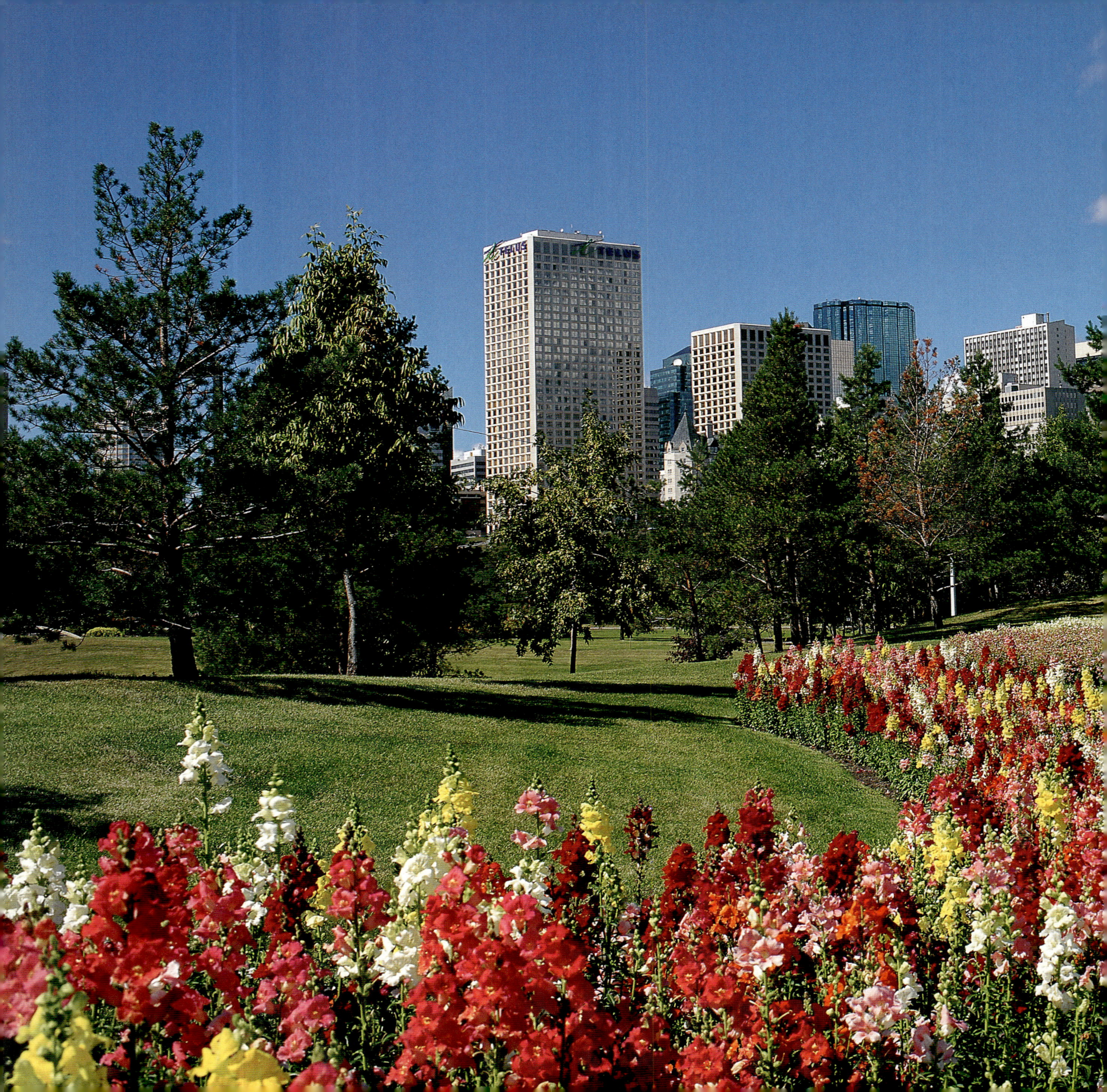
TELUS

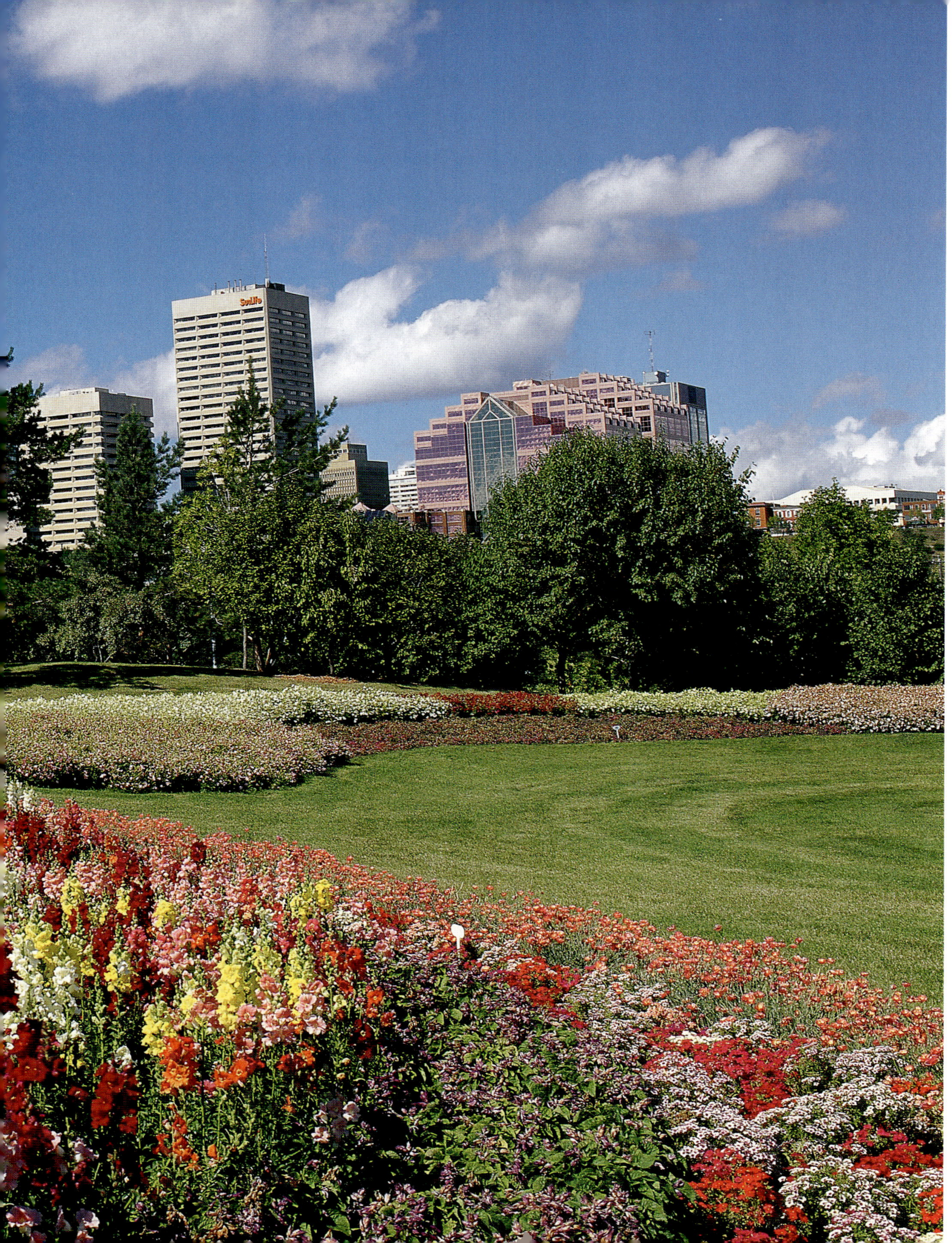

Though the first Europeans arrived centuries before, Edmonton was not incorporated until 1904. A year later, the city was named capital of the newly created province of Alberta.

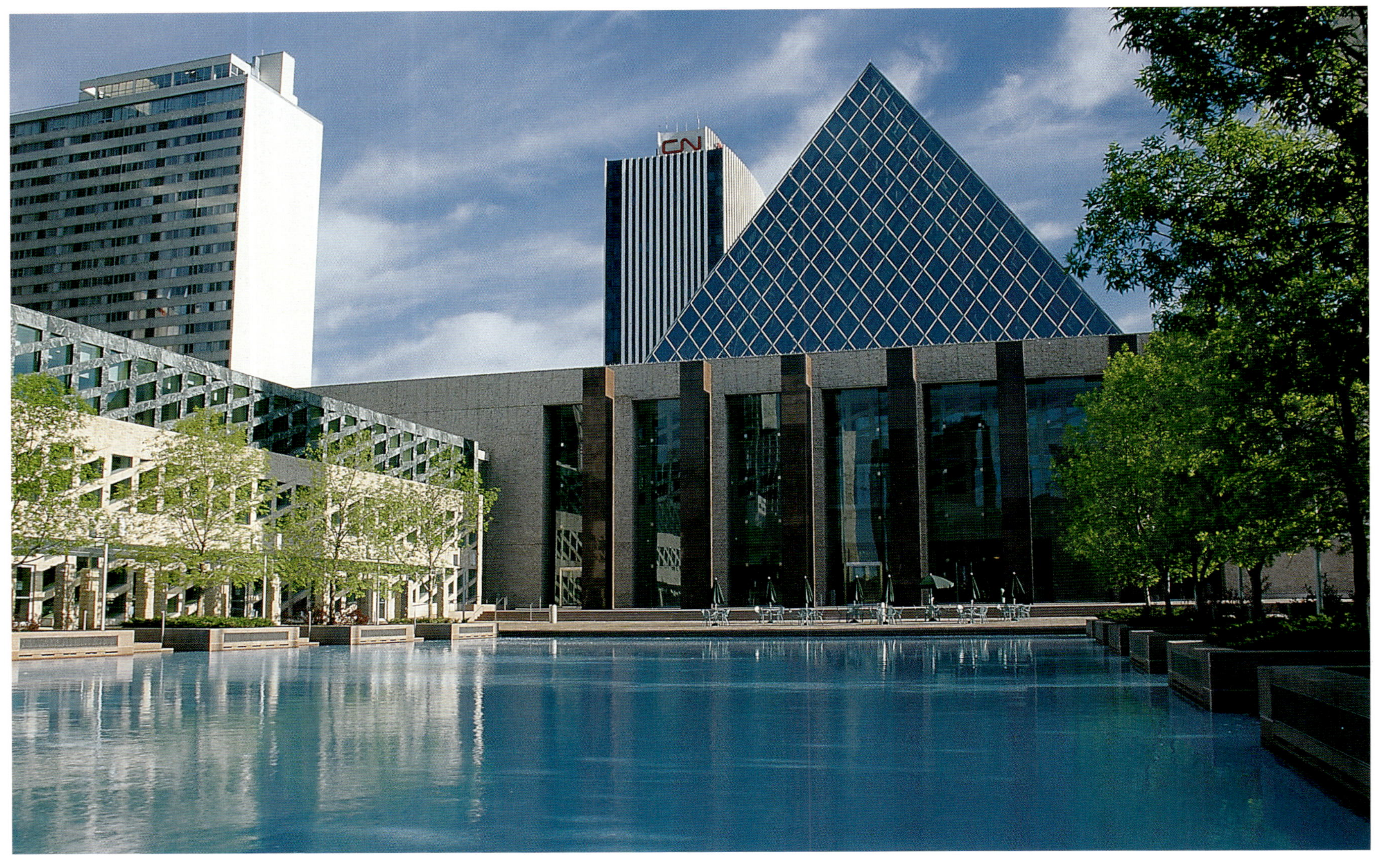

Two glass pyramids and numerous skylights in the roof of City Hall allow natural light to stream into the rooms below. The largest of these is the City Room, where works by Alberta artists offer original perspectives on the province's culture.

Summerfest, a gathering of jugglers, magicians, musicians, and performers who defy categorization, is Edmonton's annual festival of street entertainment. For a week each July, city residents are treated to outrageous costumes, incredible acts, and activity on every corner.

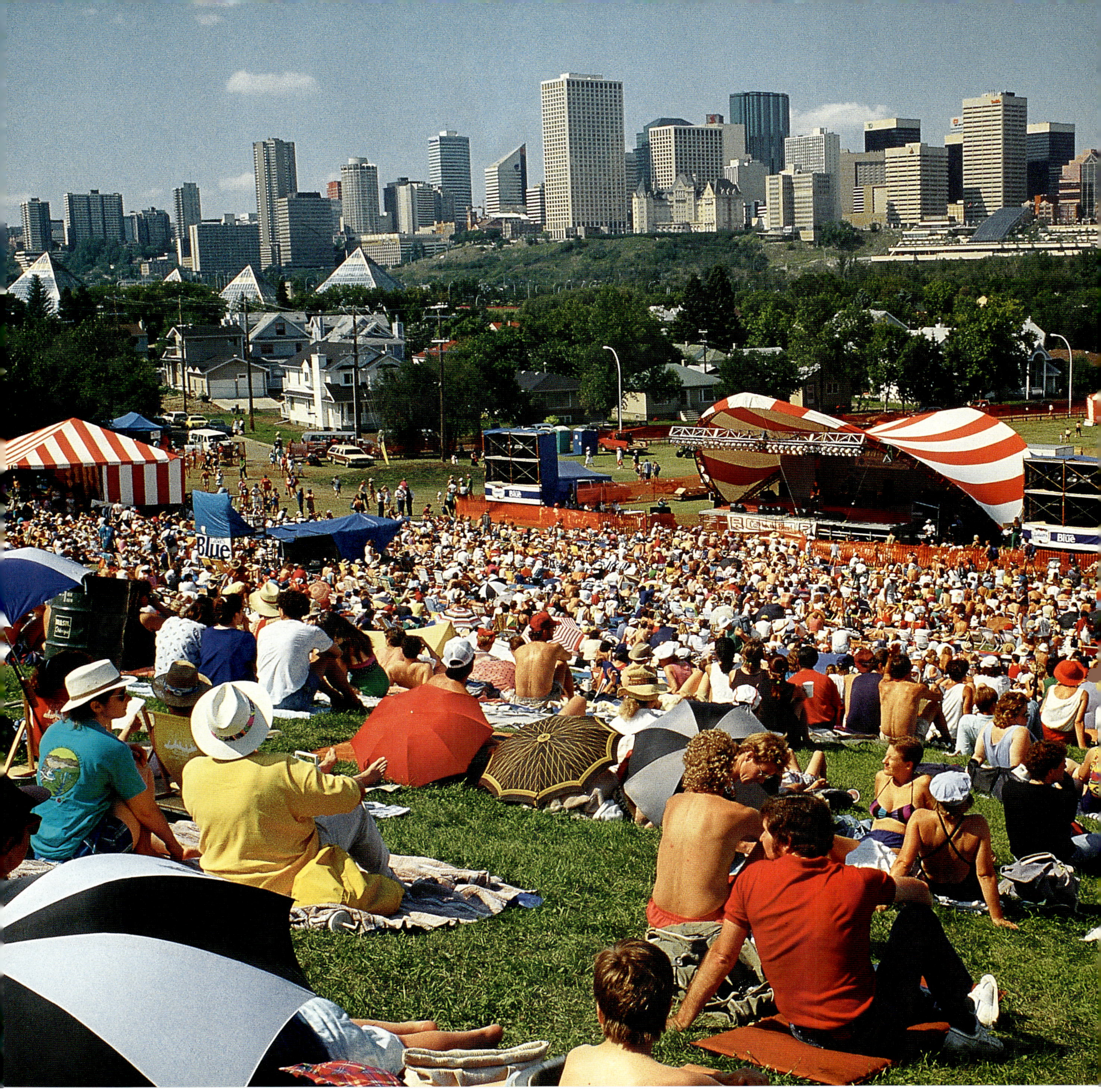
Blue

The architect scoured the globe for the best stone to use in the Legislative Buildings, including Vancouver Island granite and sandstone from Calgary and Ohio. To create the rotunda, Jeffers imported more than 2,000 tonnes (2,200 tons) of marble from Quebec, Italy, and the United States.

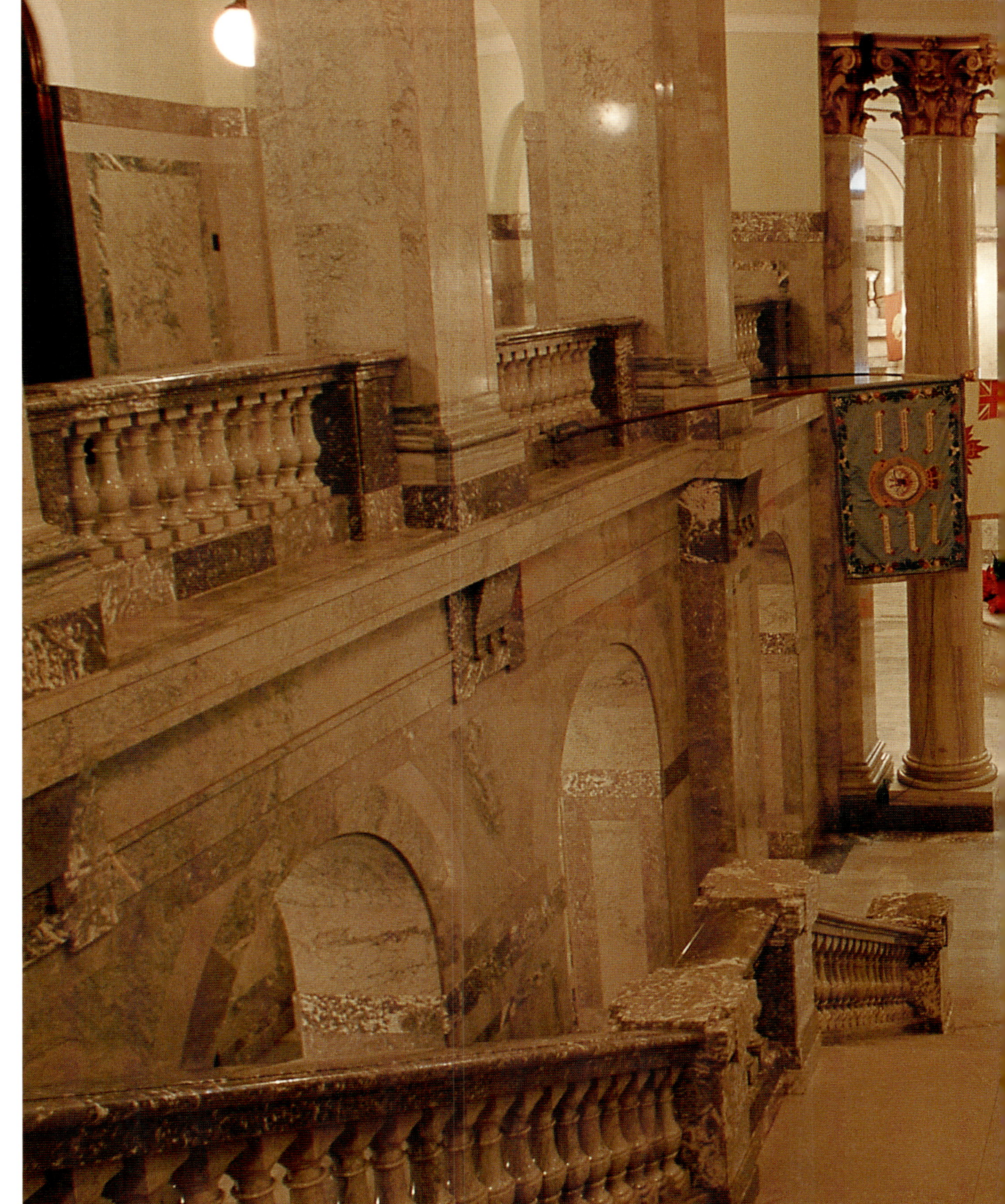

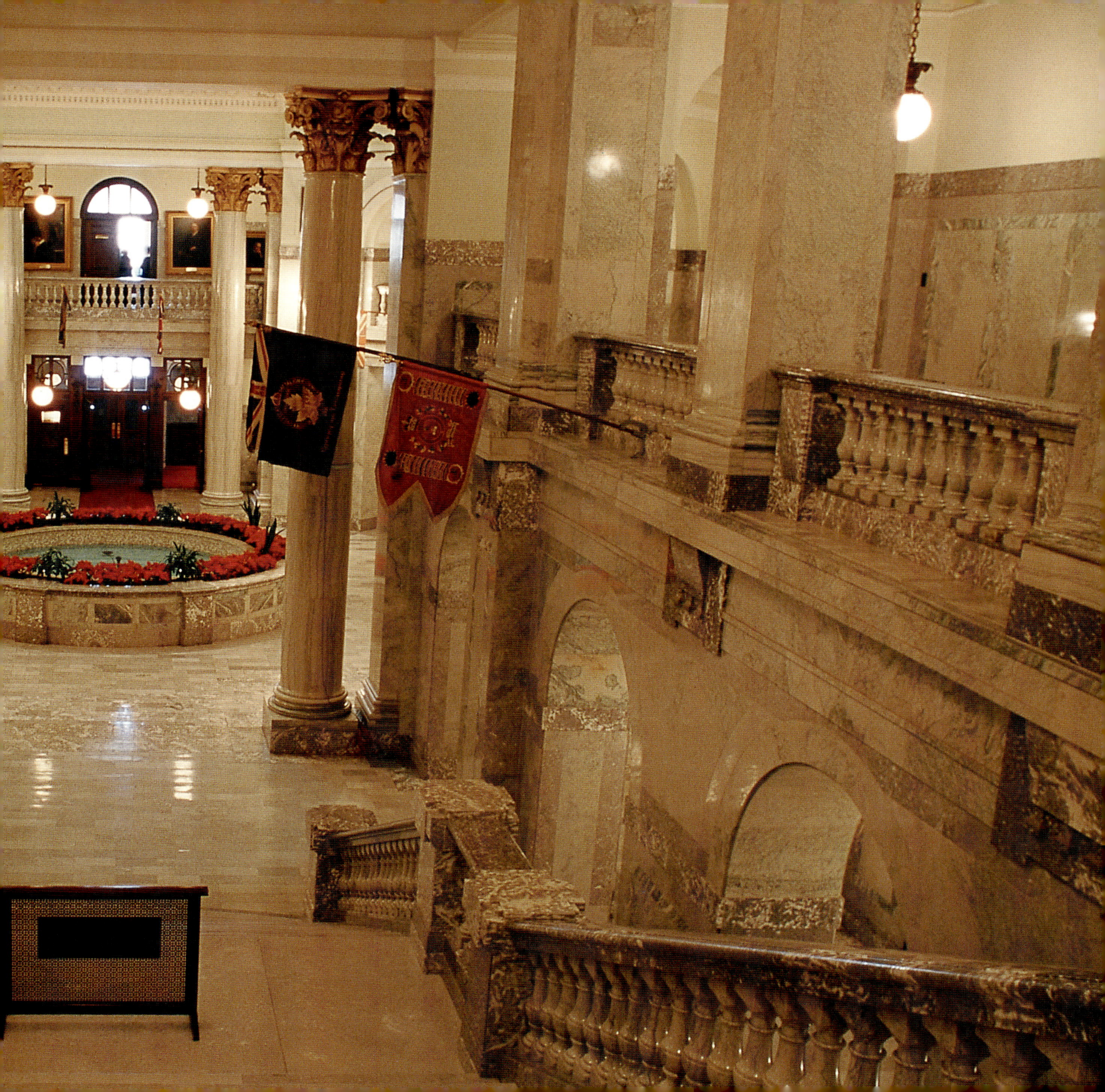

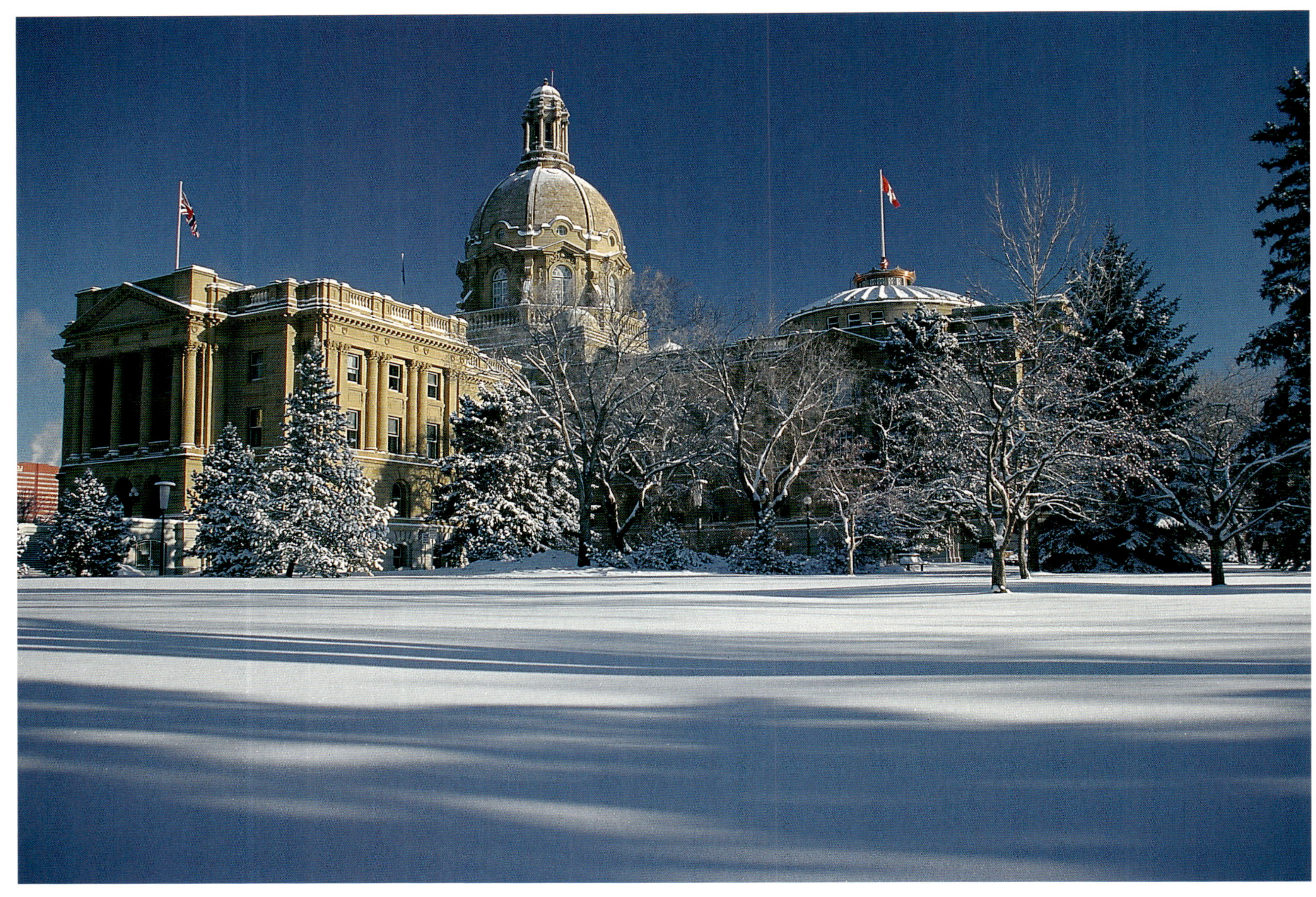

After Alberta became a province, the first meeting of the government was held in one of Edmonton's community skating rinks. Eager to move to more stately quarters, members convened in the new Legislative Buildings in 1911, before construction was complete.

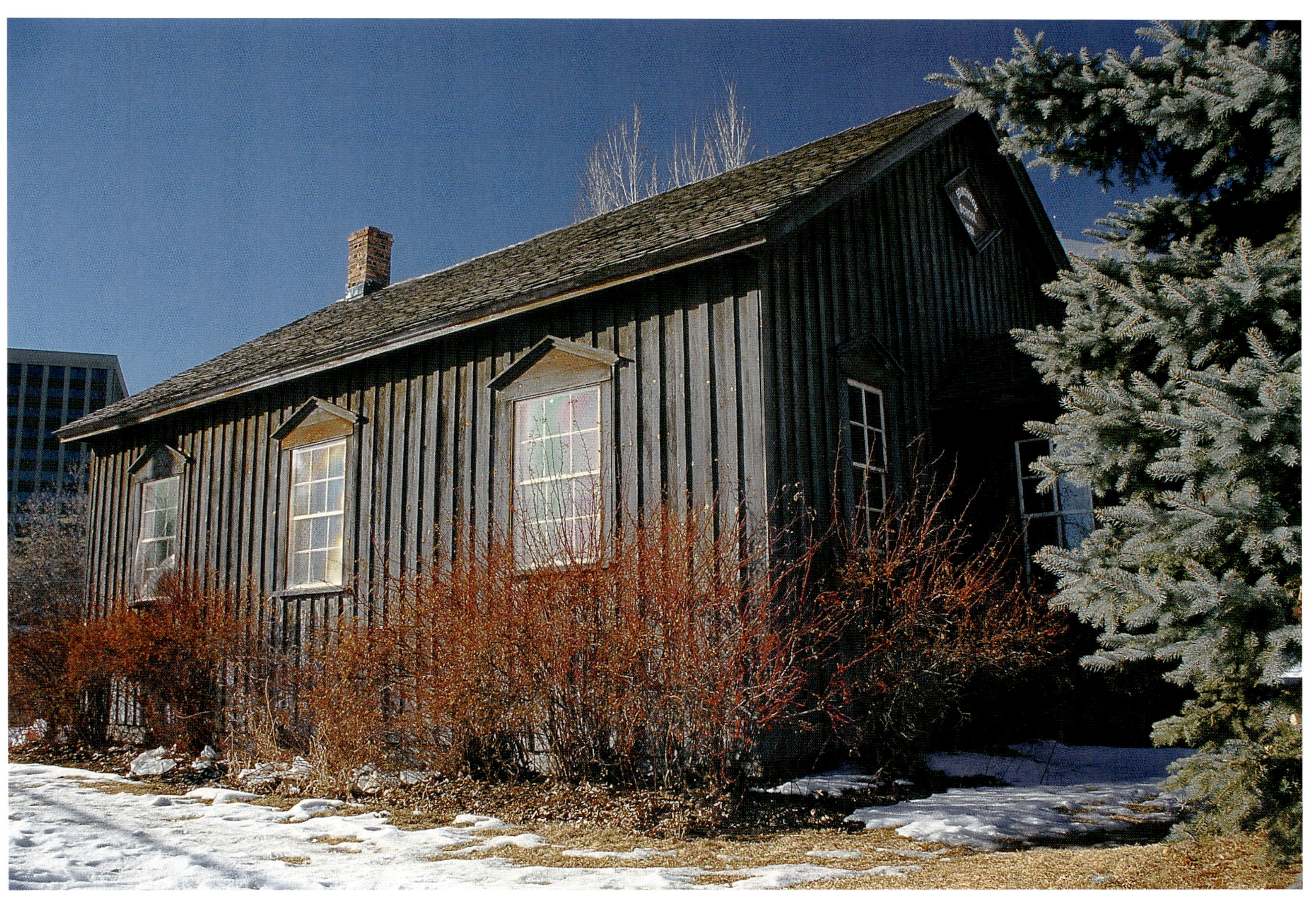

Edmonton's first schoolhouse was named for Dr.William Morrison MacKay of the Hudson's Bay Company. Unfortunately, the school's name was first engraved as "McKay Avenue School" in 1881 and the misspelling was never corrected.

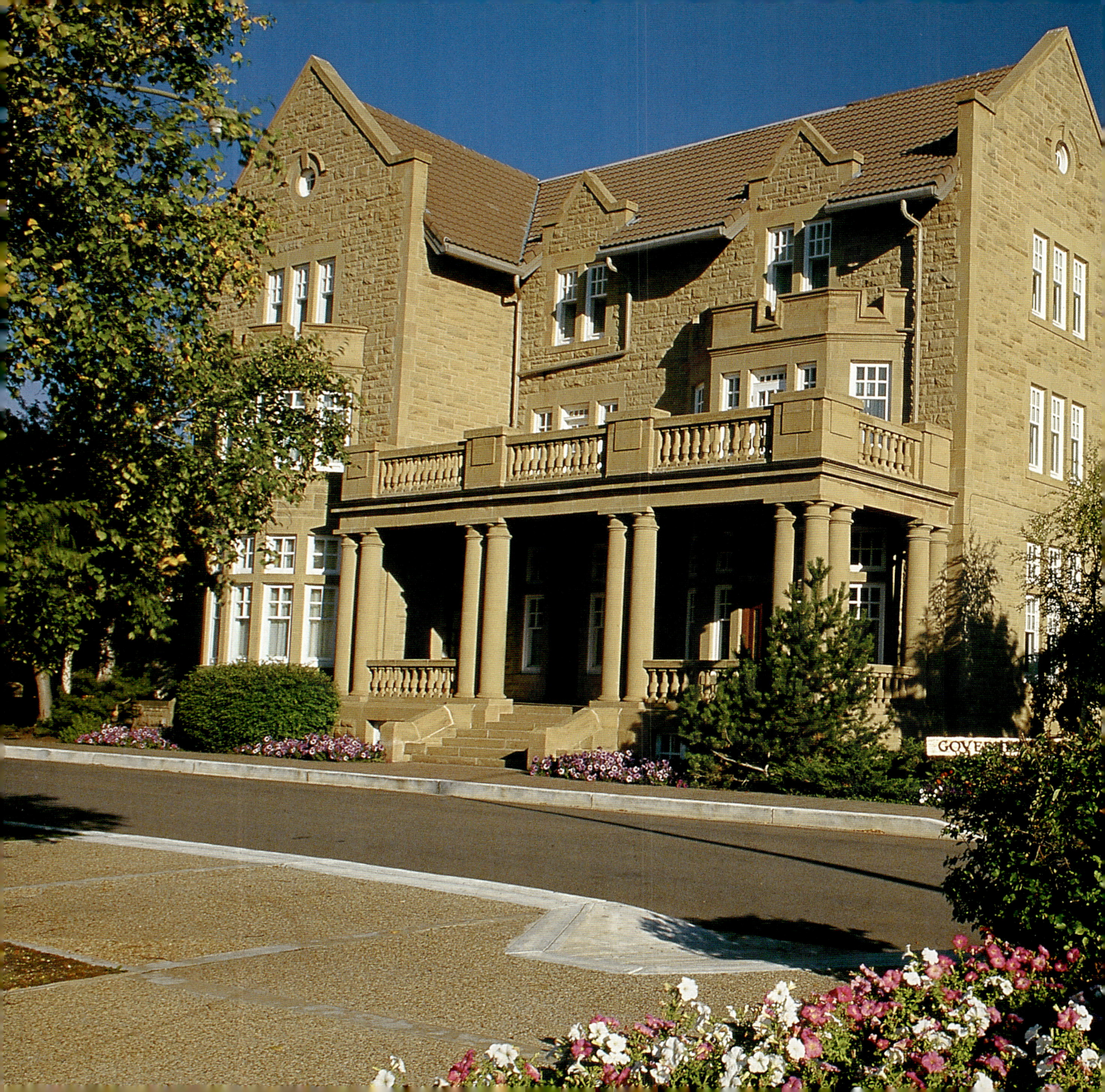

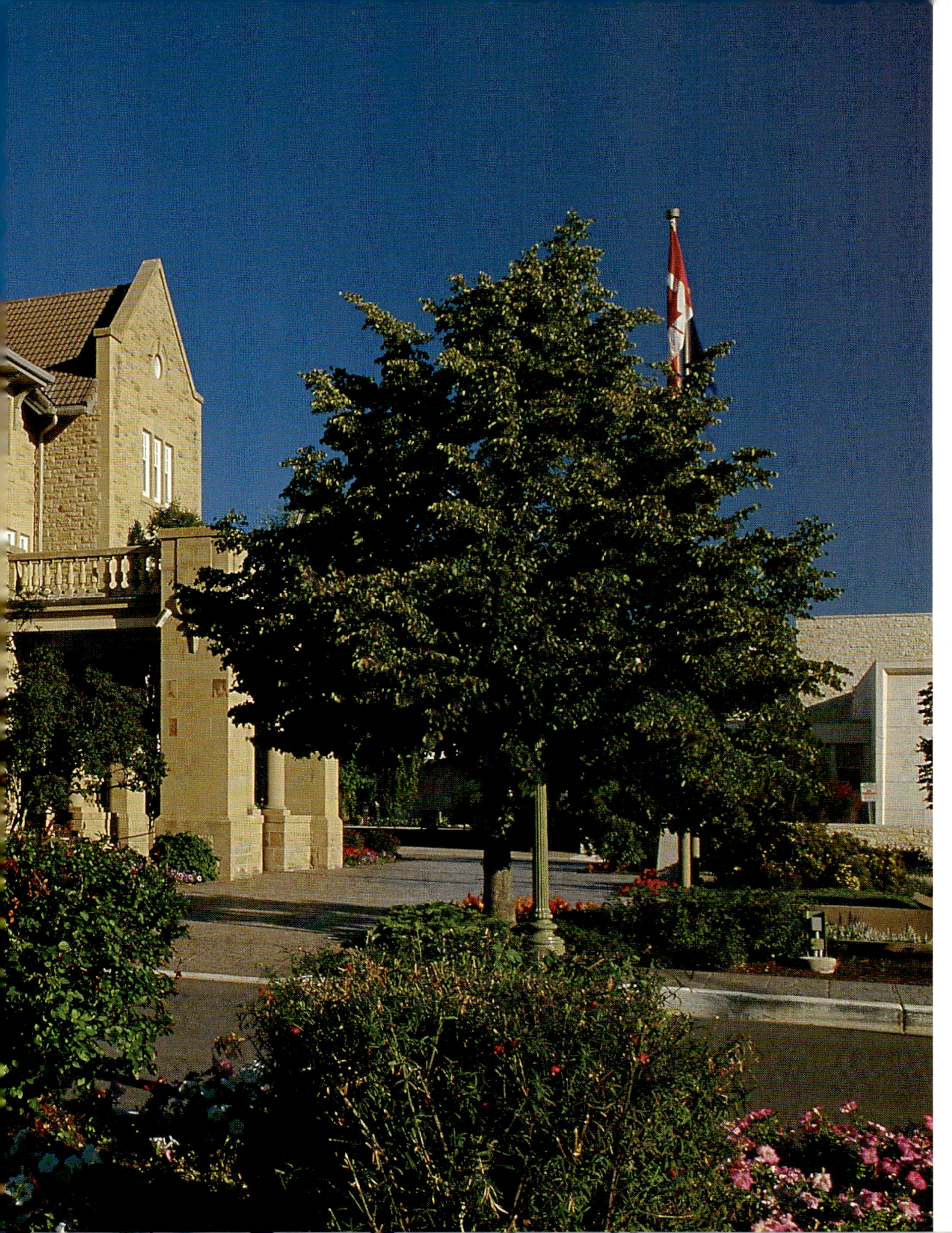

Government House was built in 1913 and served as the home of Alberta's lieutenant-governors for 25 years. Later a war veterans' hospital, the sandstone structure was renovated and reopened in 1976. It now hosts state functions and government conferences.

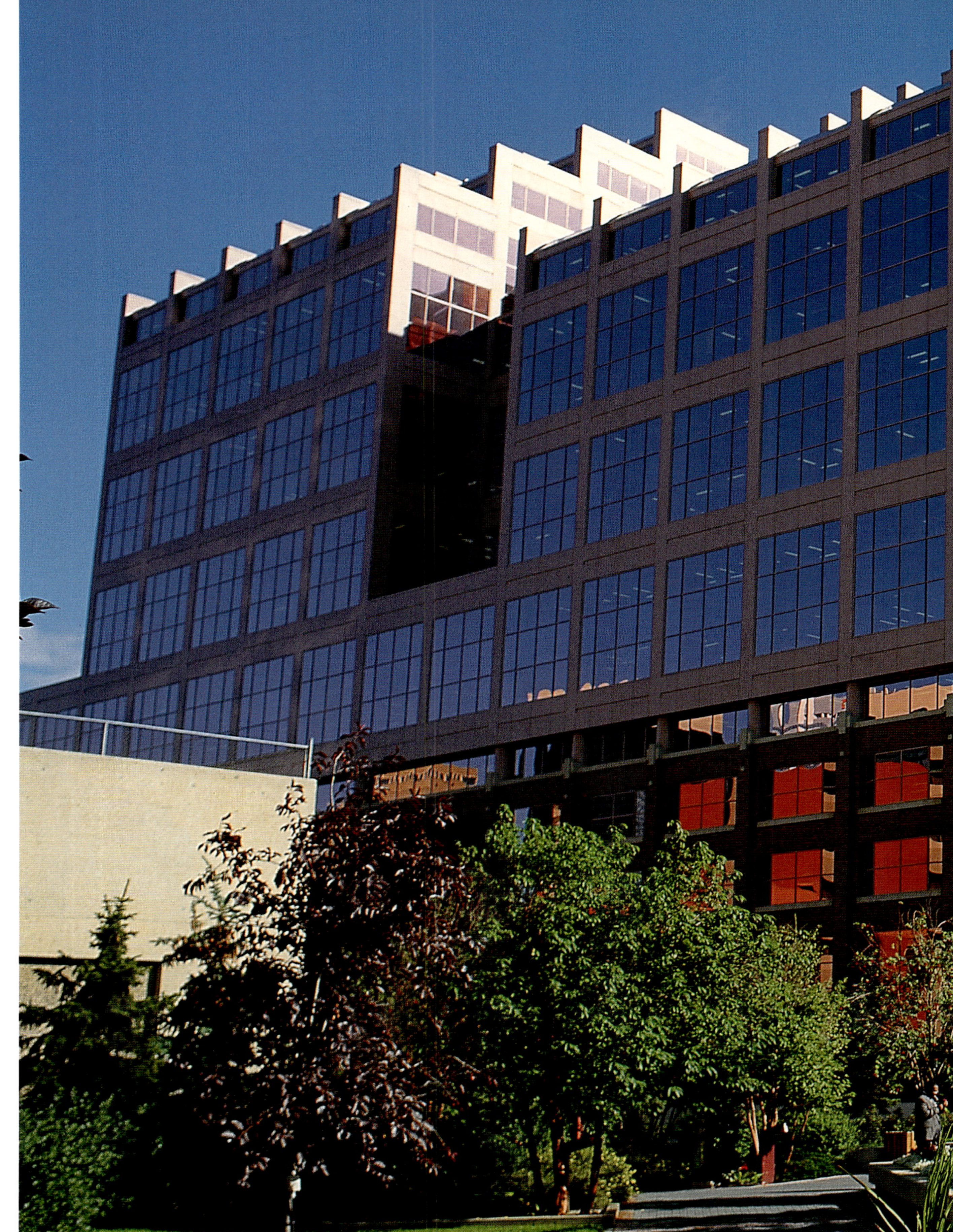

Canada Place is home to the federal government's Edmonton offices. Completed in 1986, the 16-storey building was a striking addition to the city skyline and won several awards for its design.

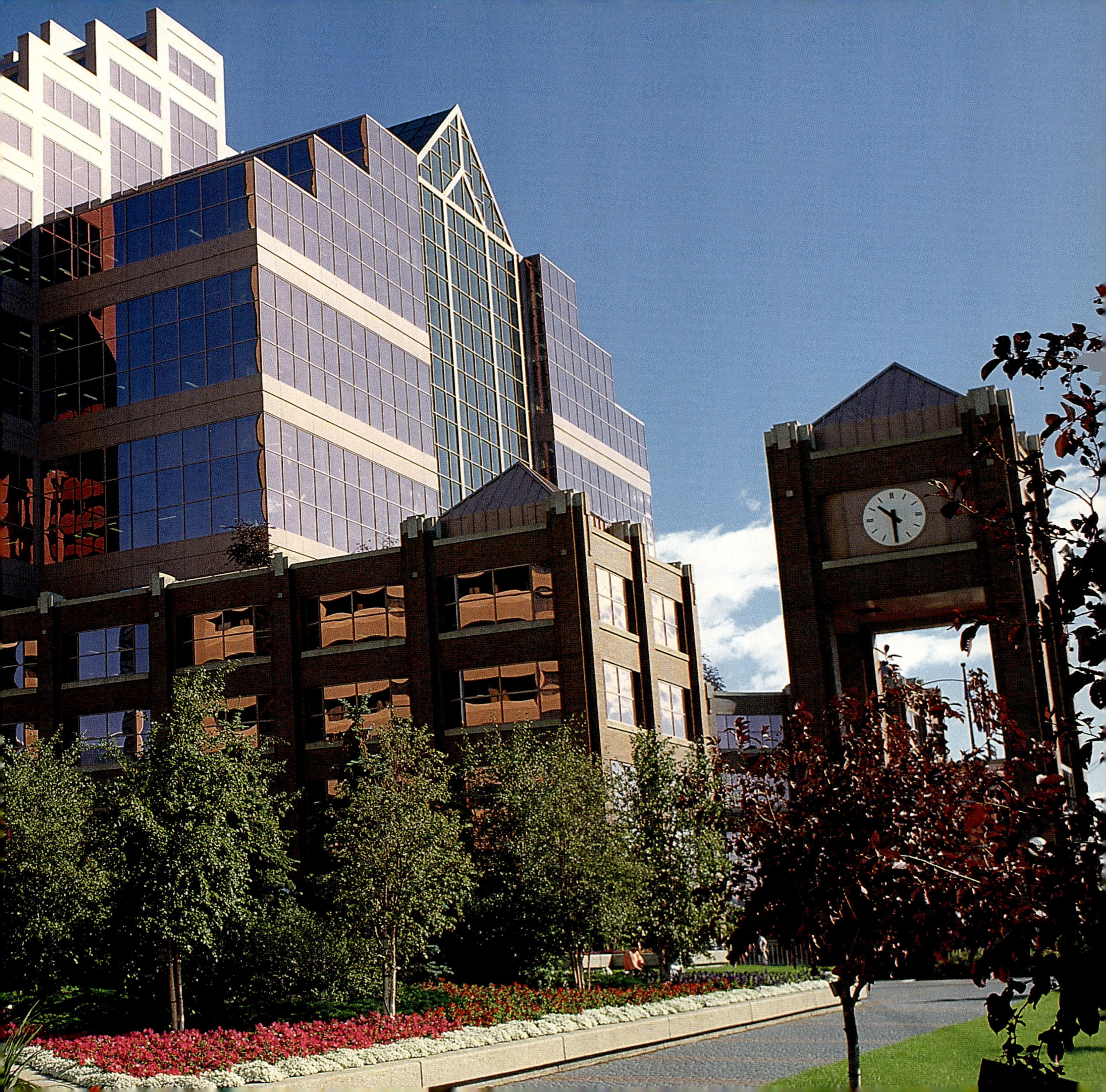

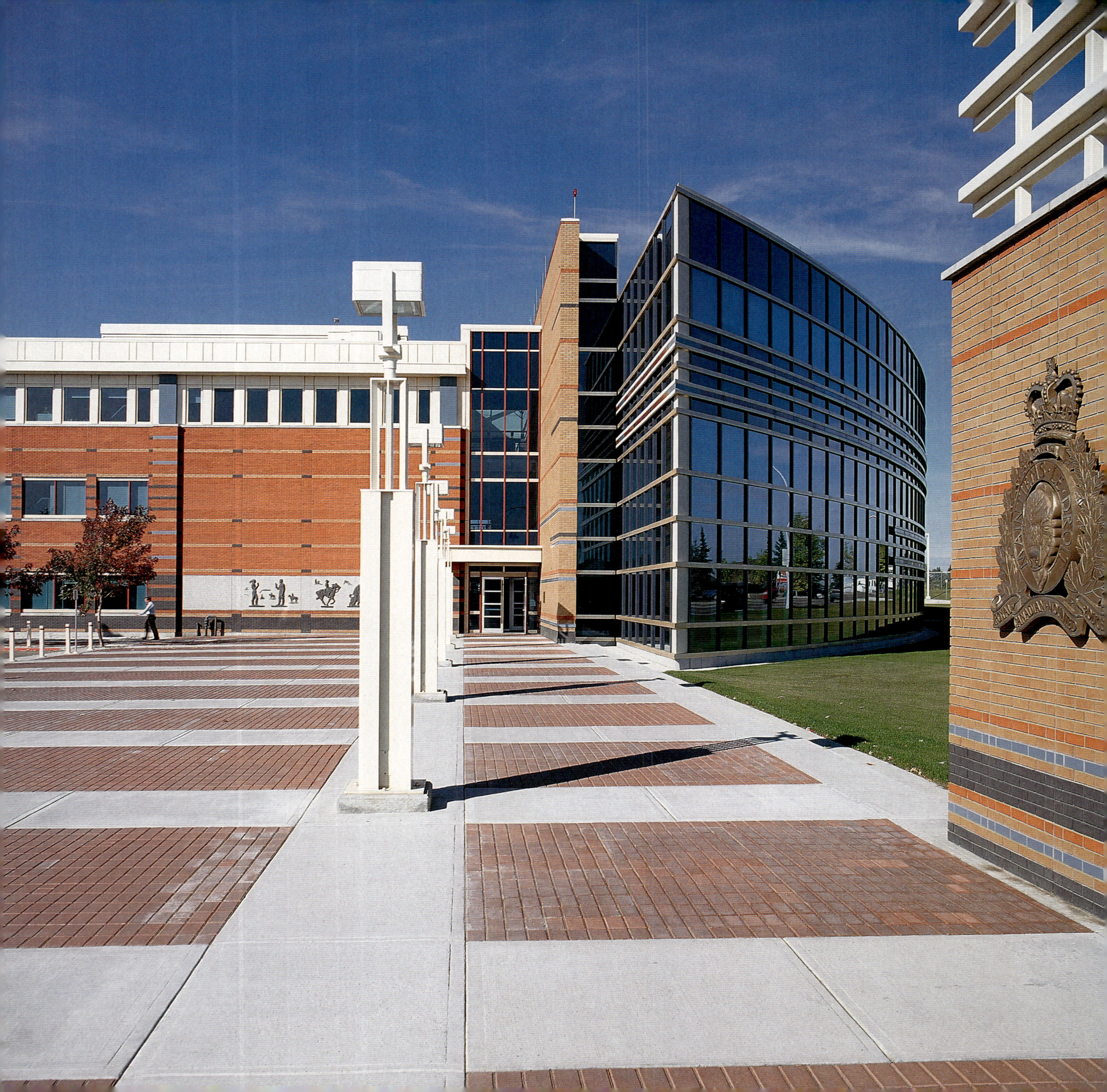

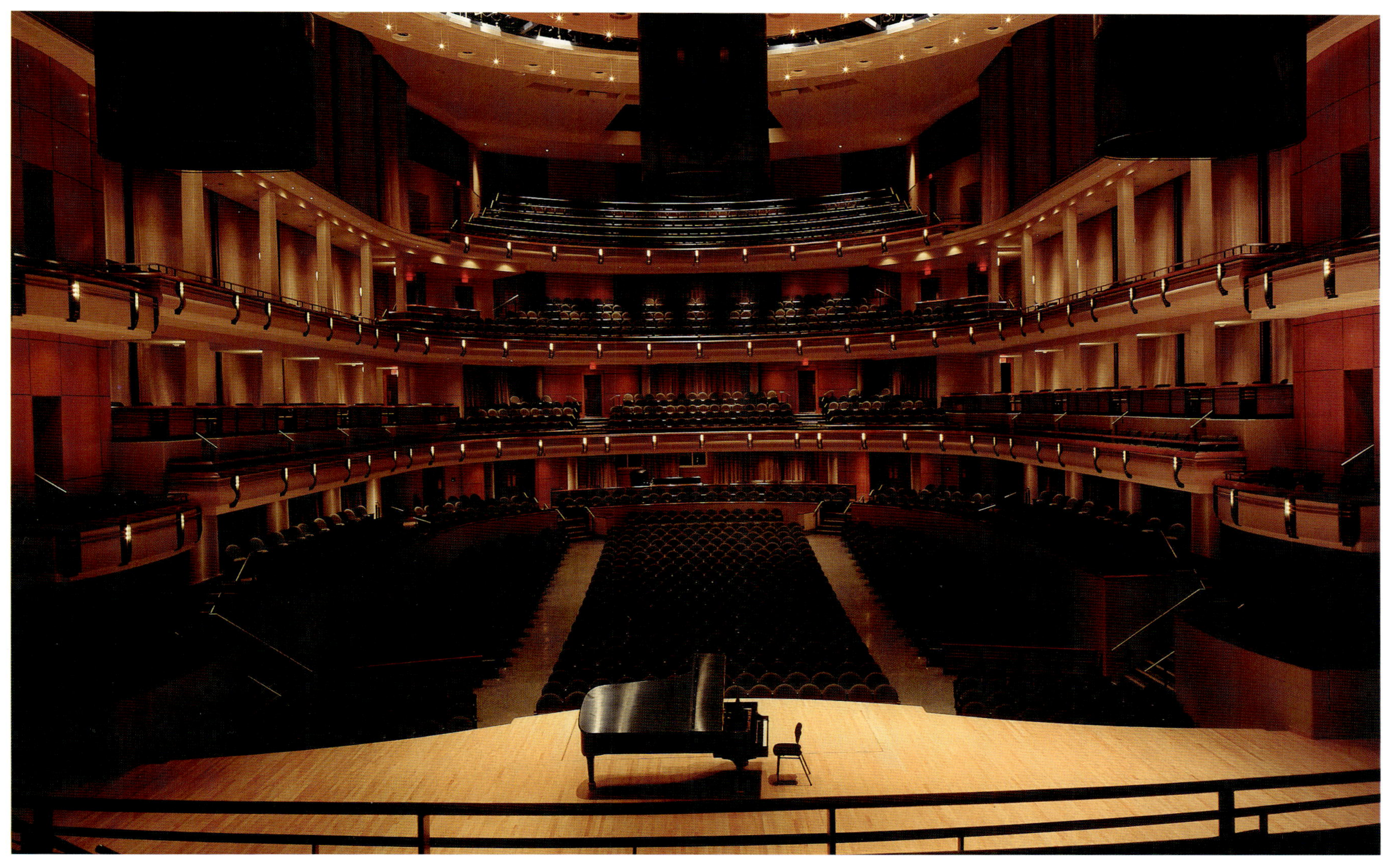

The Francis Winspear Centre for Music opened in 1997, thanks to a $6 million contribution — the largest amount ever donated to a Canadian performing arts venue — by Dr. Francis Winspear. Home to the Edmonton Symphony Orchestra, the centre also hosts many speakers and performers.

The RCMP Headquarters in Edmonton stand proudly, part of a long history of policing dating to 1874, when the North-West Mounted Police arrived here under the leadership of Inspector W.D. Jarvis. His 22 men worked to establish order in the fur trade and end the whiskey trade.

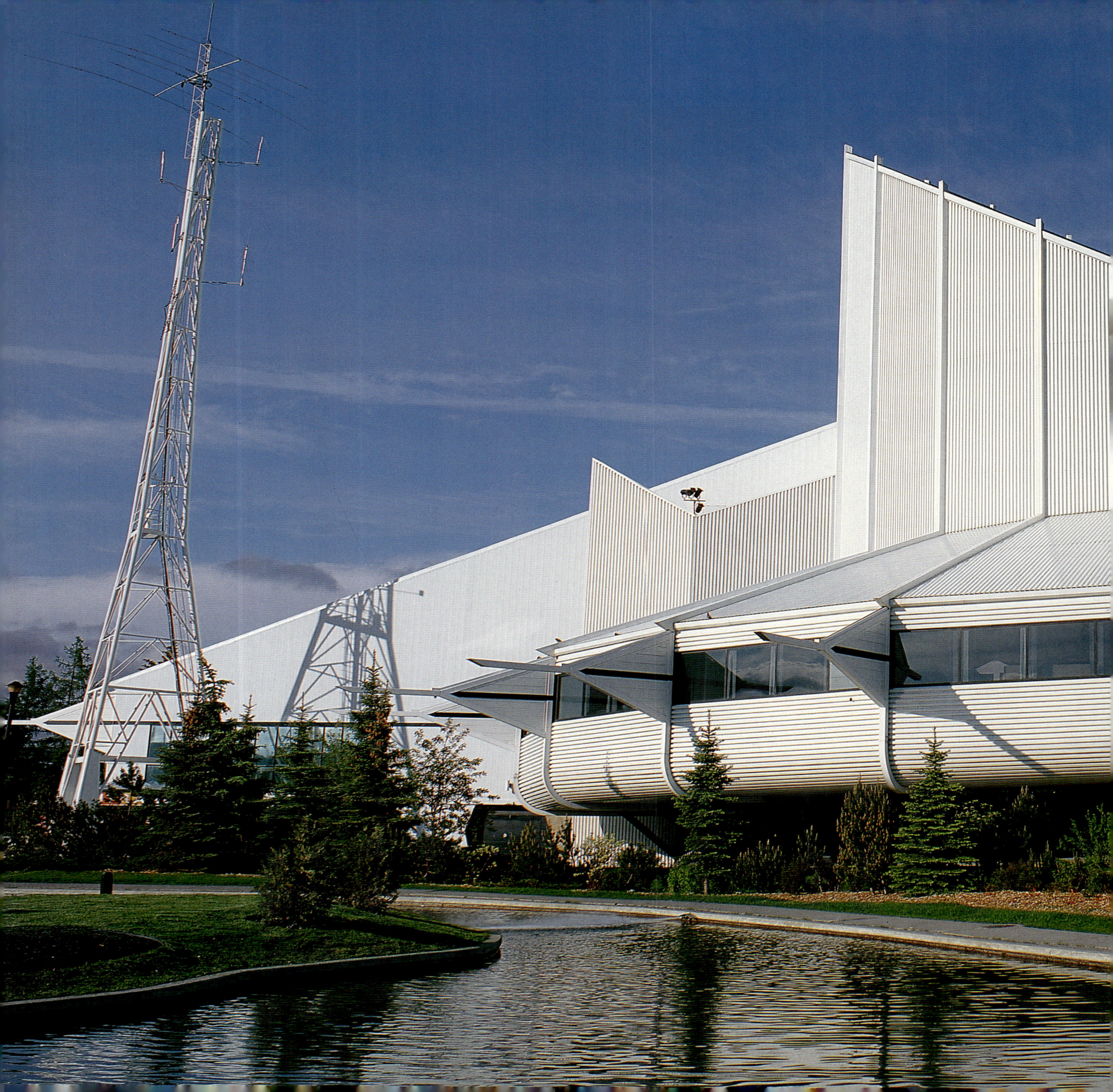

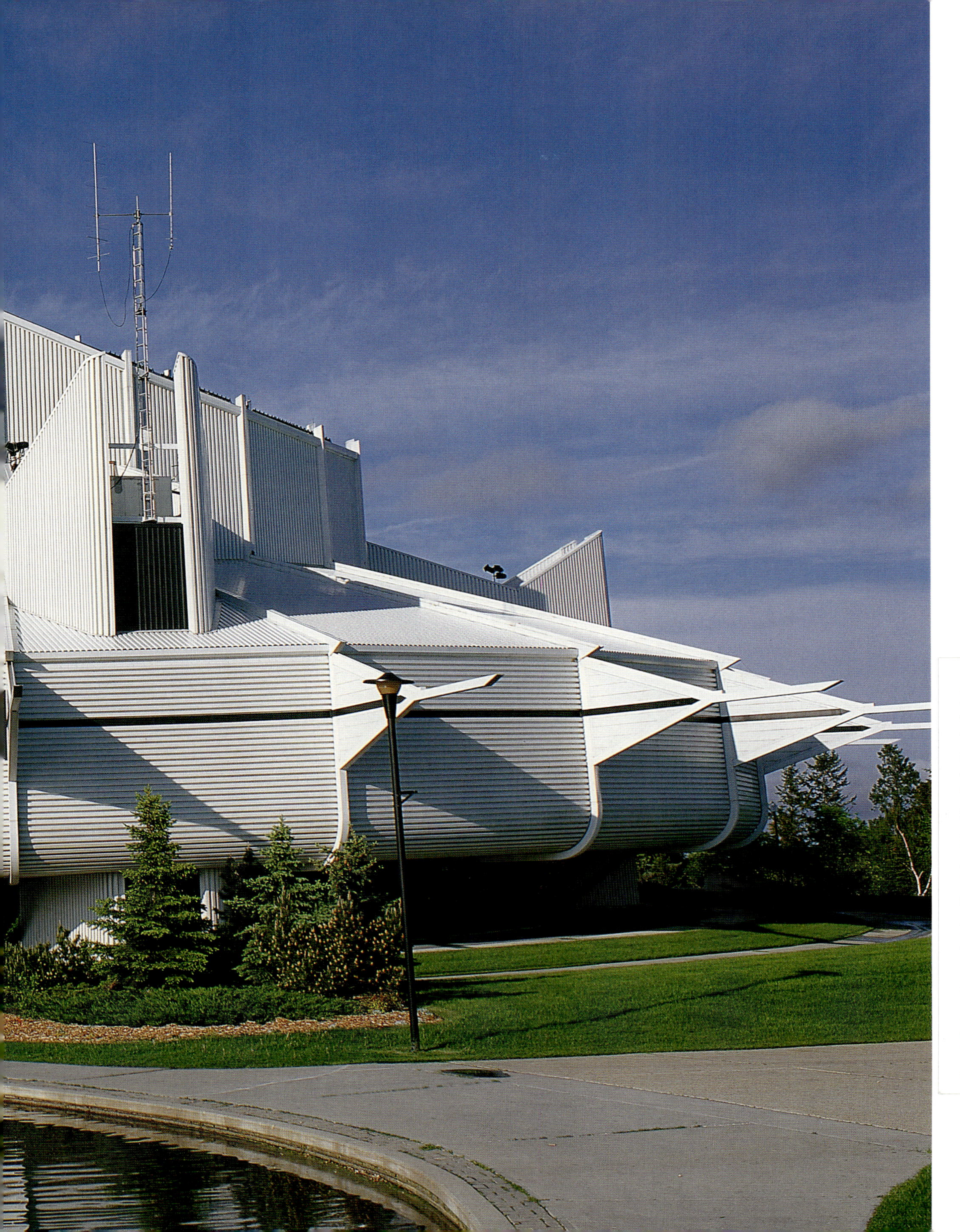

Métis architect Douglas J. Cardinal designed the Edmonton Space and Science Centre to visually "unfold," reflecting the achievements of the human race. The centre includes an observatory, an IMAX theatre, learning galleries, and more.

whiskey trade.

Since the railway and the gold seekers first arrived, Edmonton has remained a transportation hub. Today, it is the largest city on the Yellowhead Highway and bills itself as the Gateway to the North.

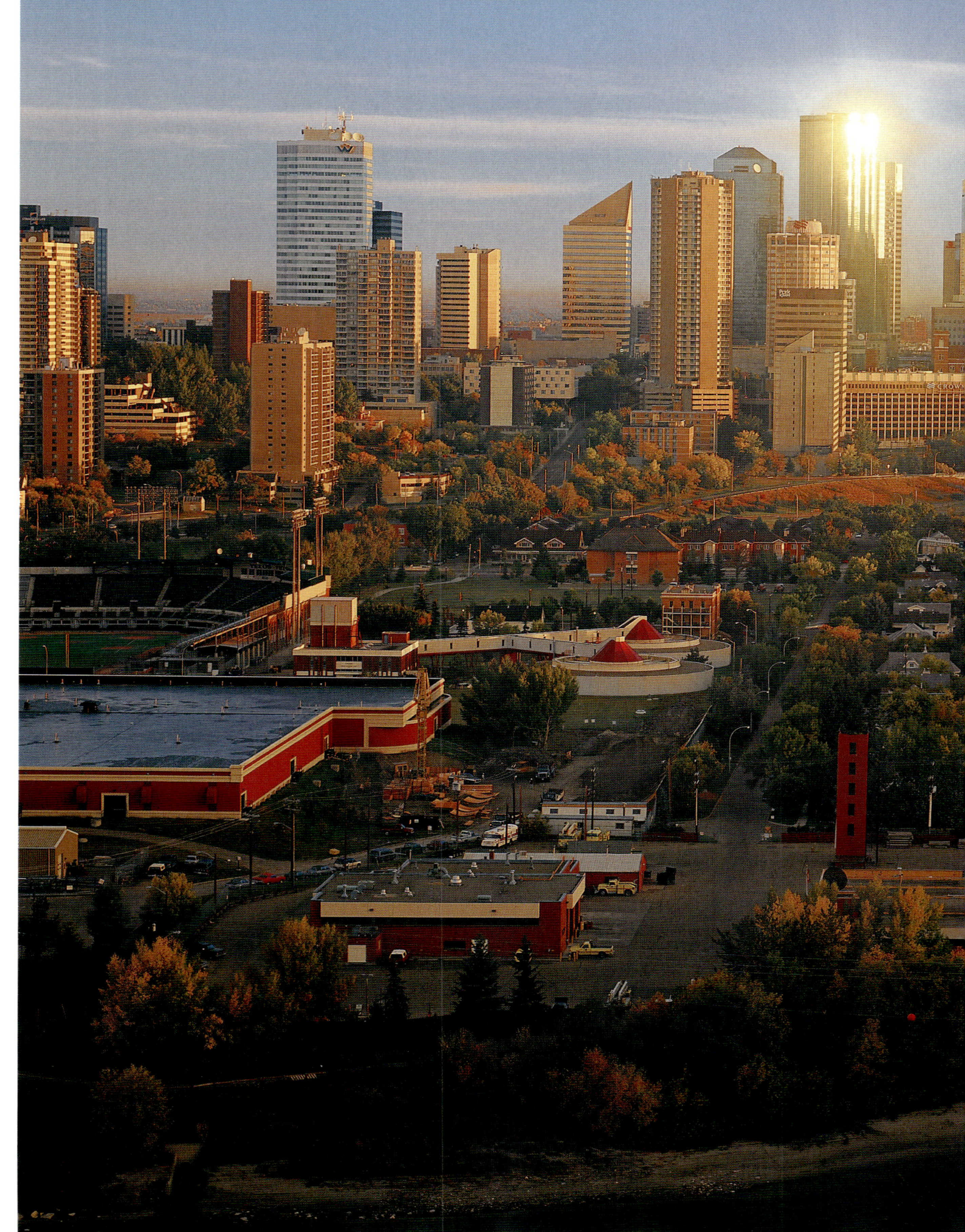

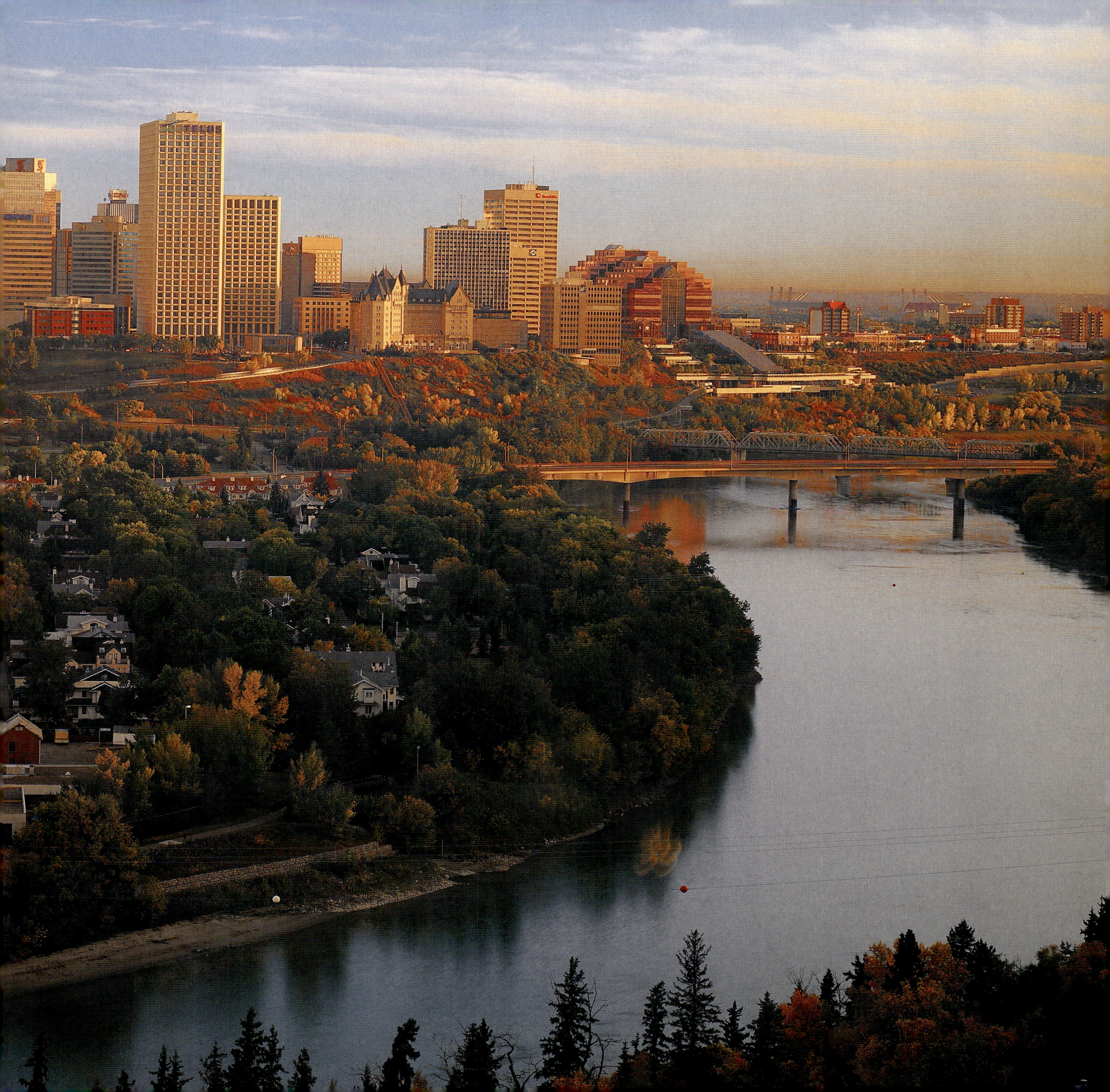

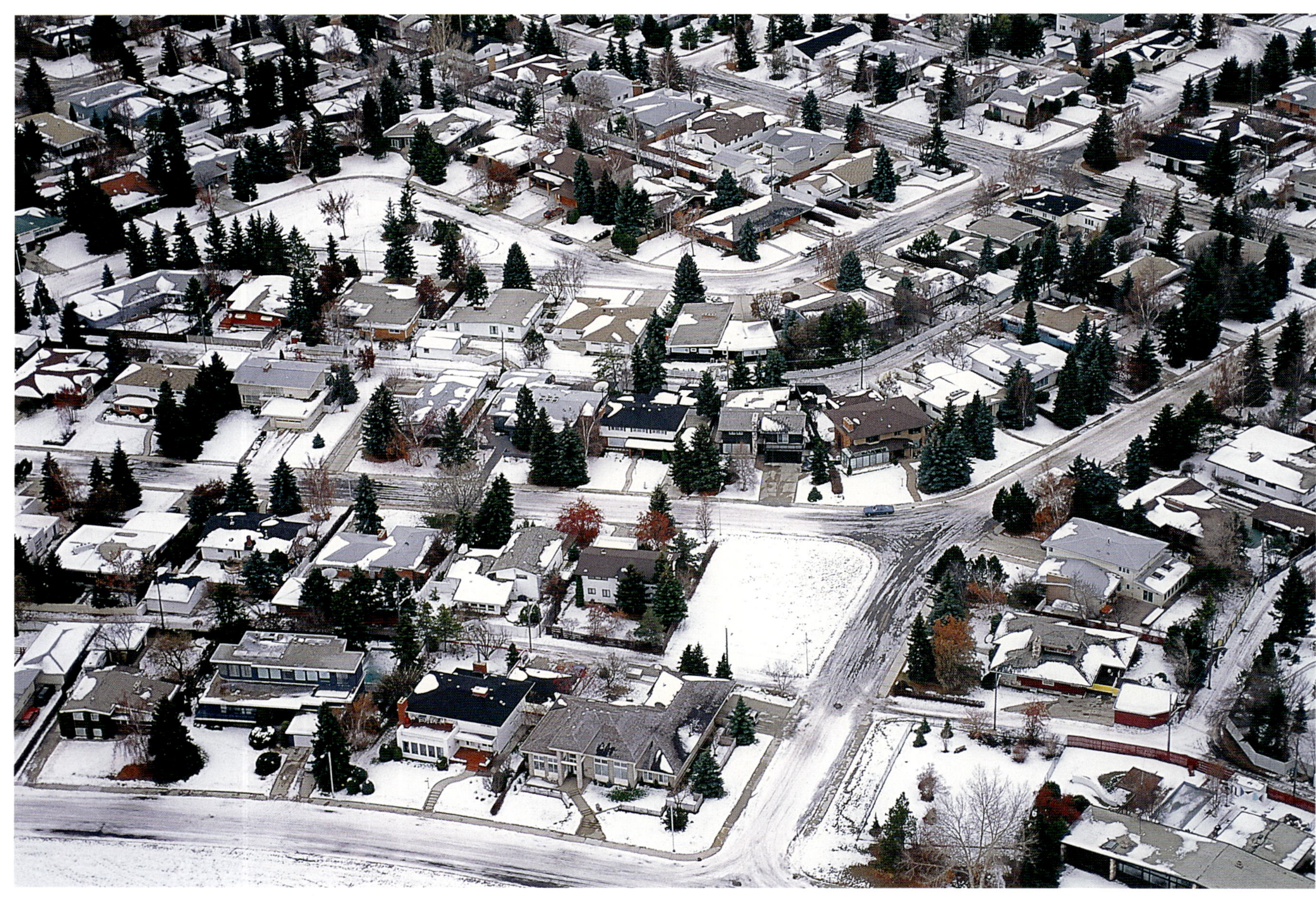

While temperatures may drop to -13°C (9°F) during an average winter, the city still enjoys plenty of sunshine — more than 2,000 hours each year.

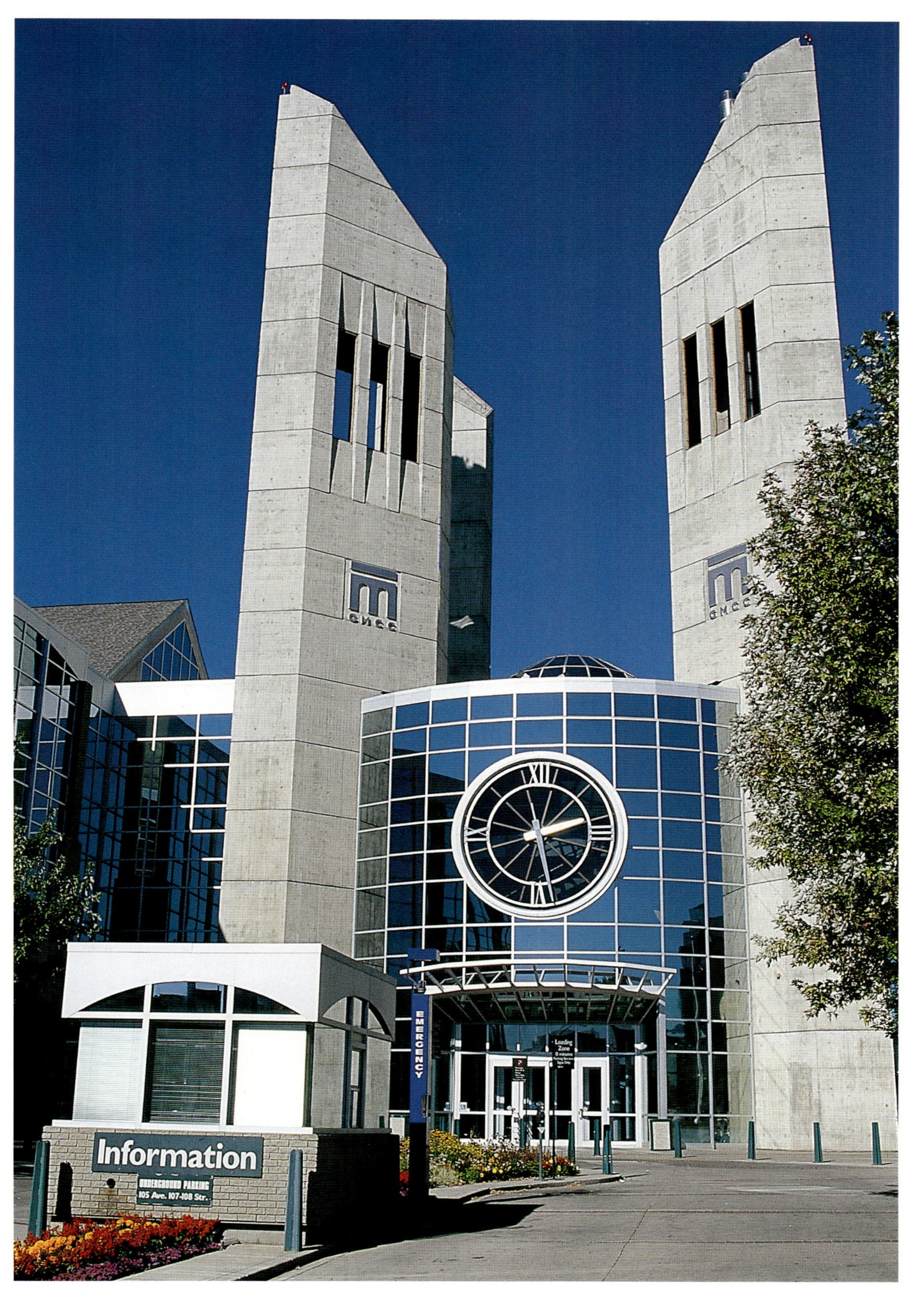

Grant MacEwan College is named for one of the city's best loved politicians. MacEwan served nine years as an alderman, three as mayor, four in the provincial legislature, and eight as the lieutenant-governor of Alberta.

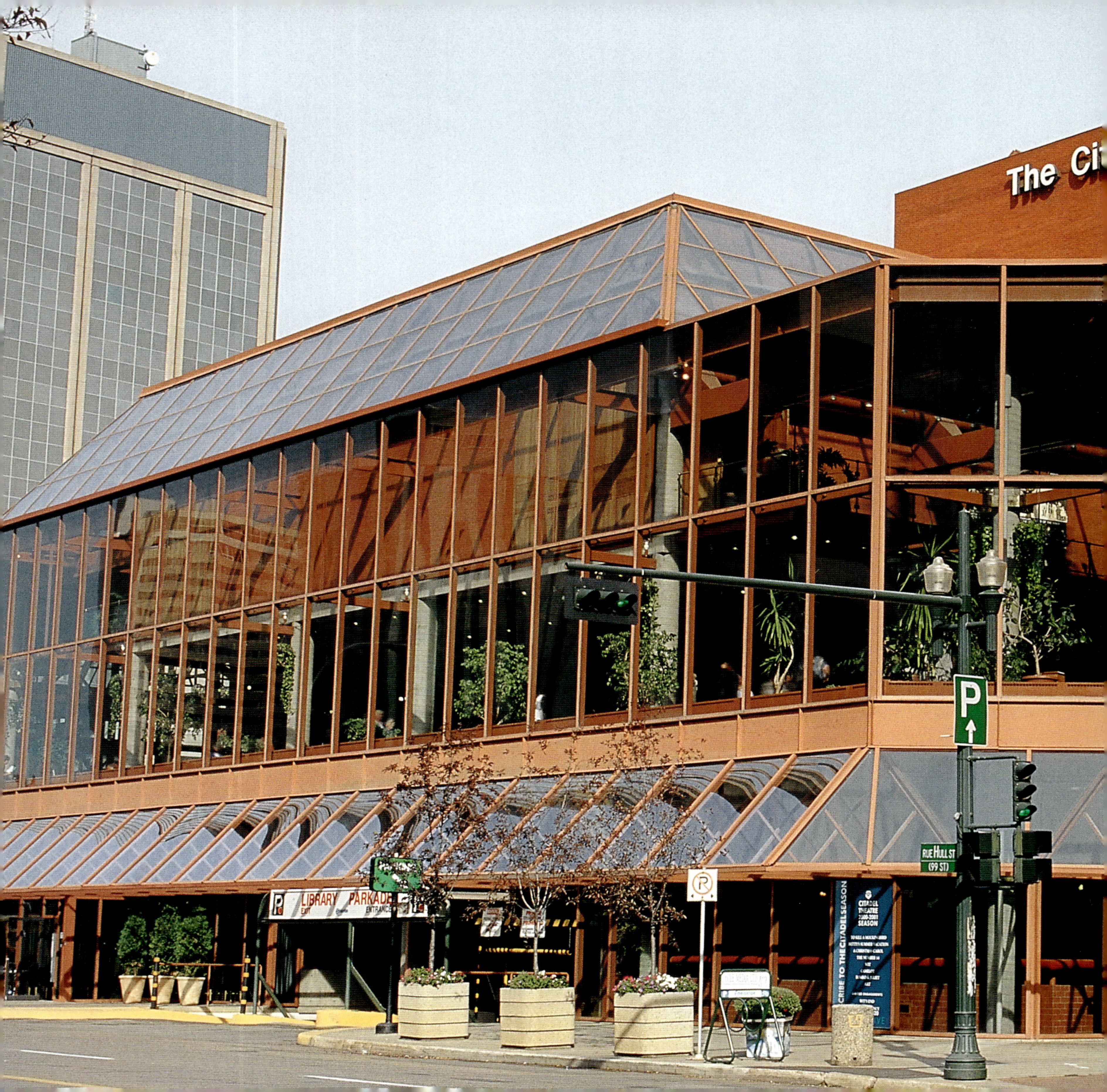
The Ci
LIBRARY PARKADE
EXIT
ENTRANCE
RUE HULL ST
(99 ST)
P

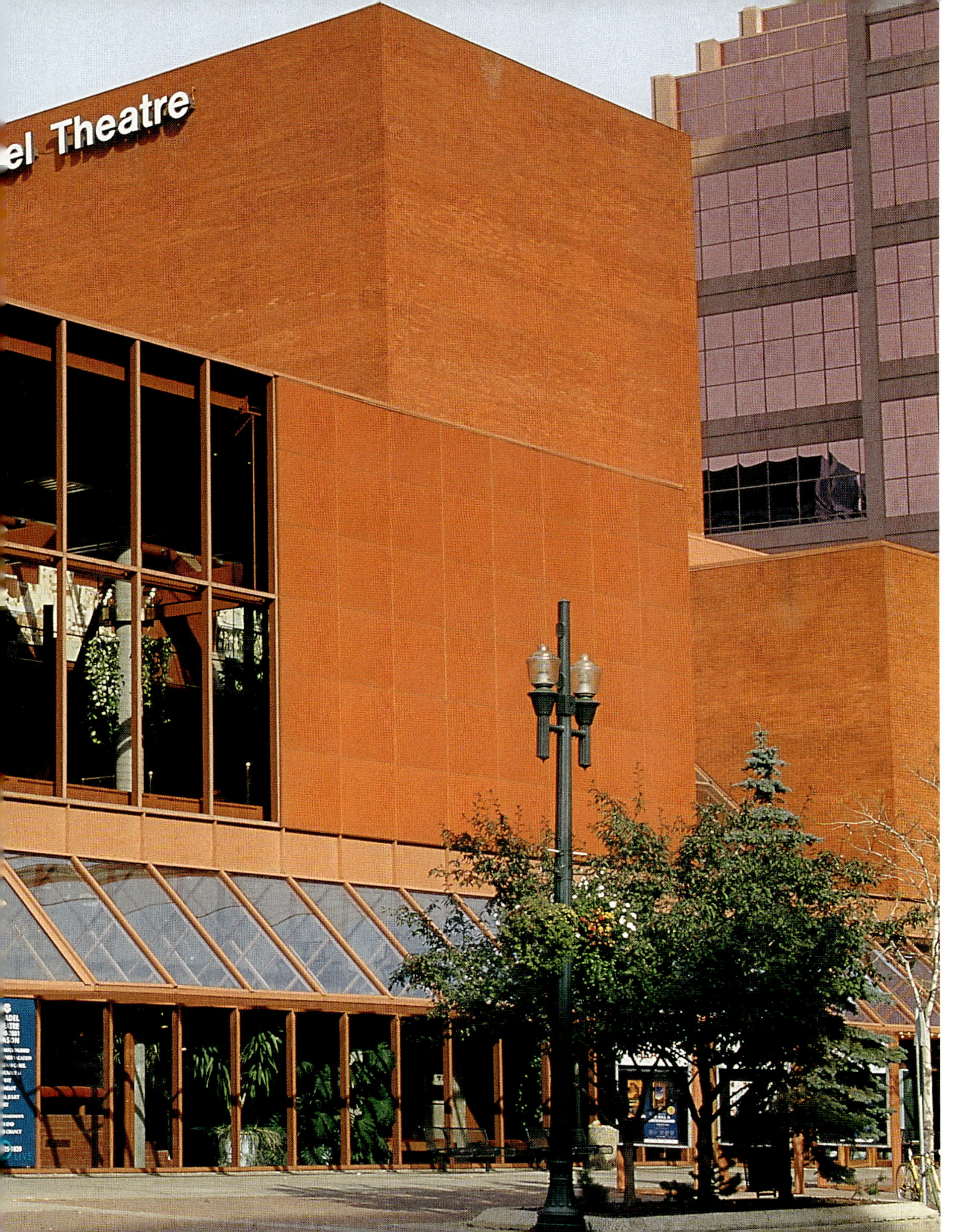

Founded in 1965, the Citadel Theatre Company moved to its present venue — one of Canada's largest performing arts centres — in 1976. Five stages, ranging from an intimate cinema to a 685-seat auditorium, provide space for productions of any size and budget.

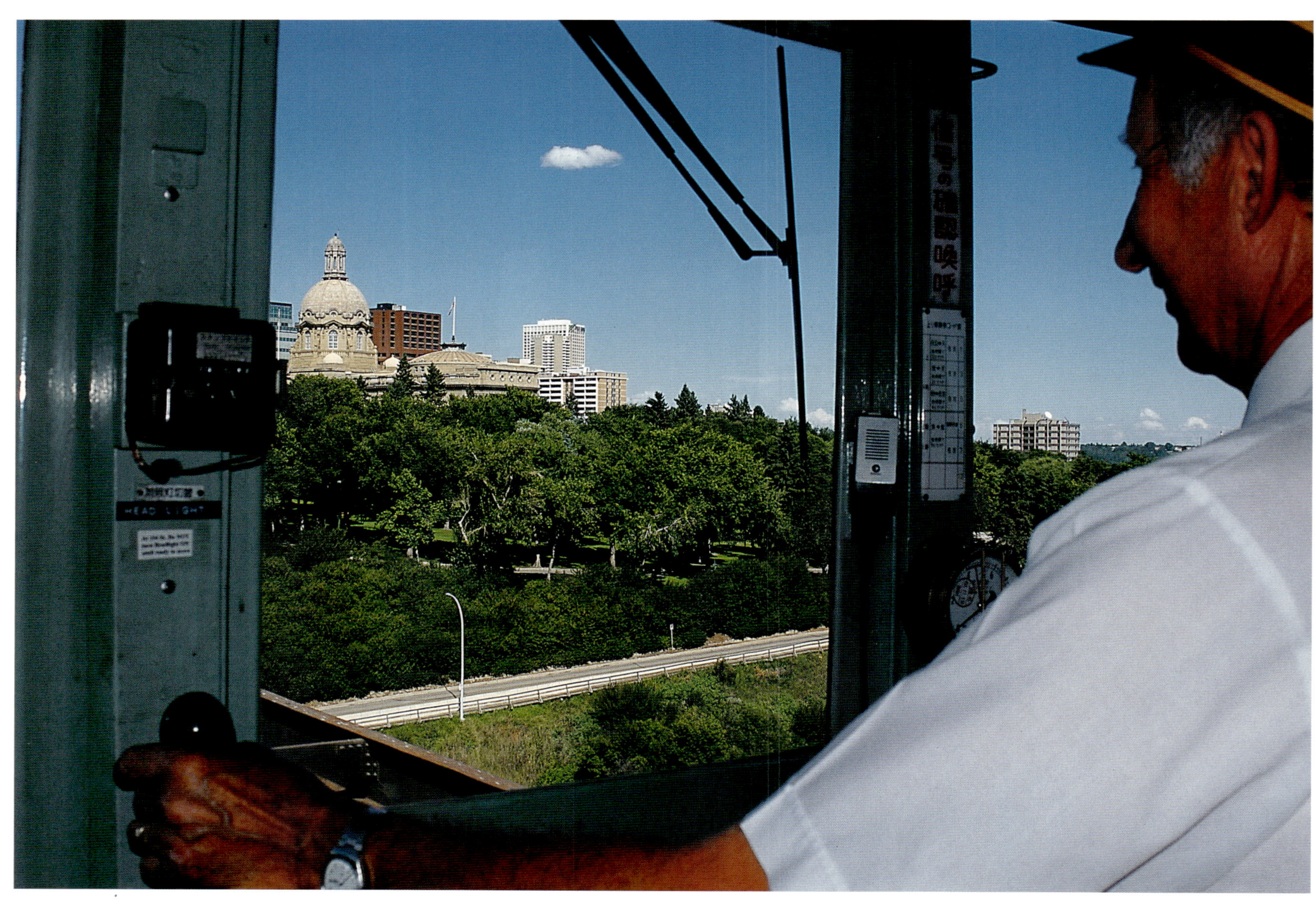

Streetcars have chugged through the city since November, 1908, when the fare was five cents. At the time, Edmonton's population was only 18,500 and this was the first prairie city to implement a public streetcar system.

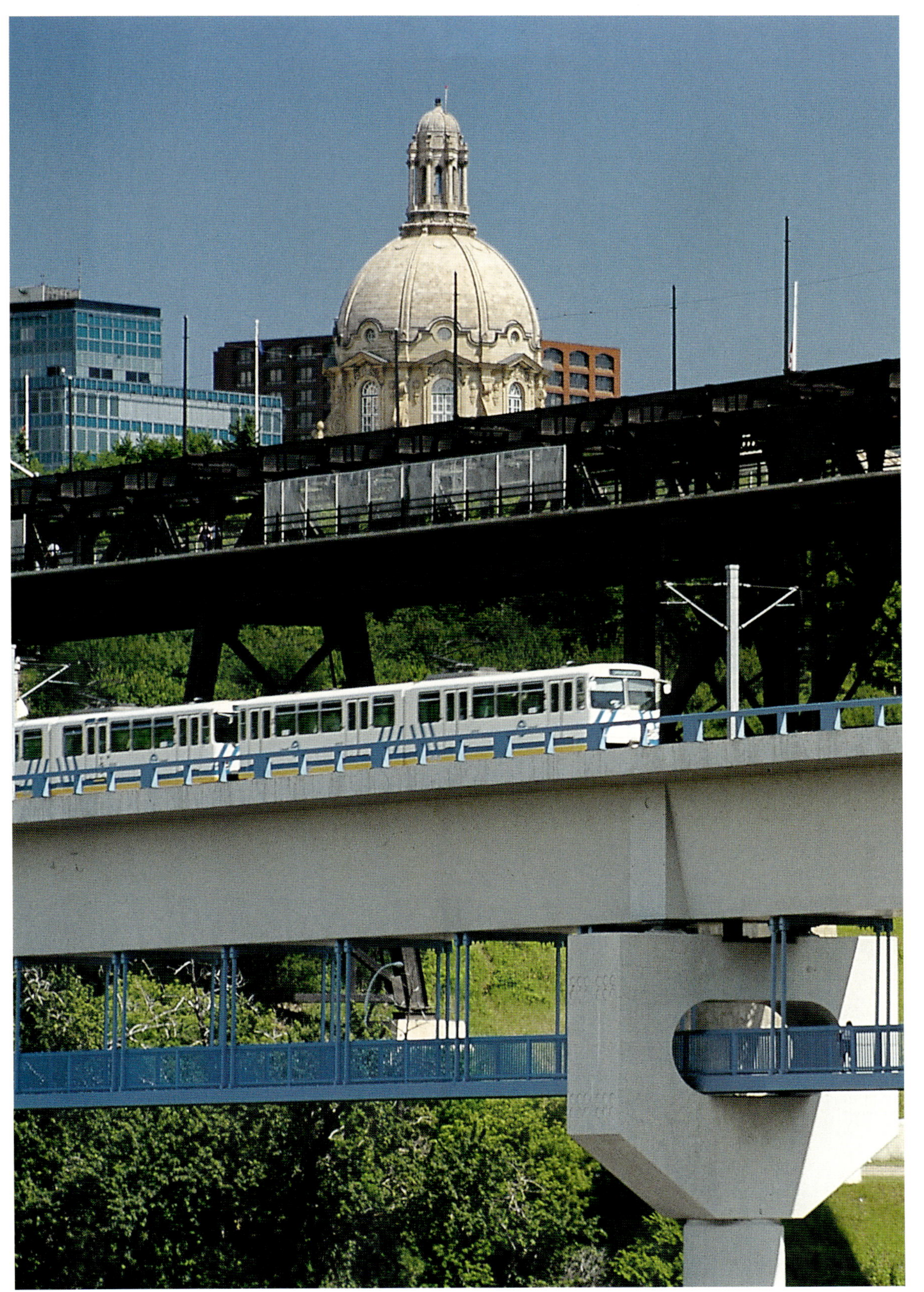

Arching 53 metres (174 feet) above the North Saskatchewan River, the High Level Bridge combines streetcar tracks and railway lines on an upper level with a roadway below. The 755-metre (2,477-foot) span was completed in 1913.

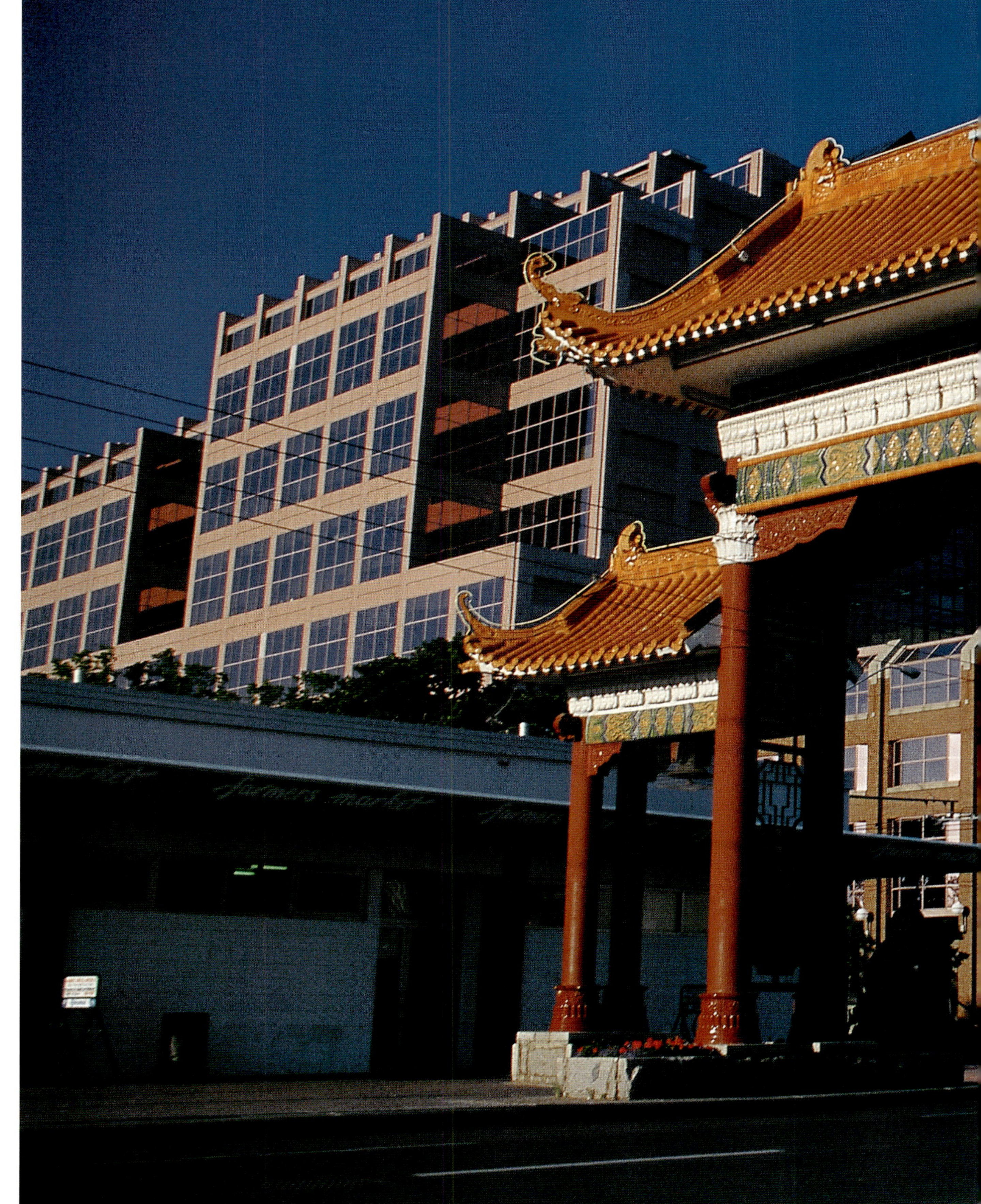

Chinatown Gate was a gift from Edmonton's sister city of Harbin, China. Artisans there designed the gate, then flew to Alberta to assemble it. The structure symbolizes the continuing friendship between the cities.

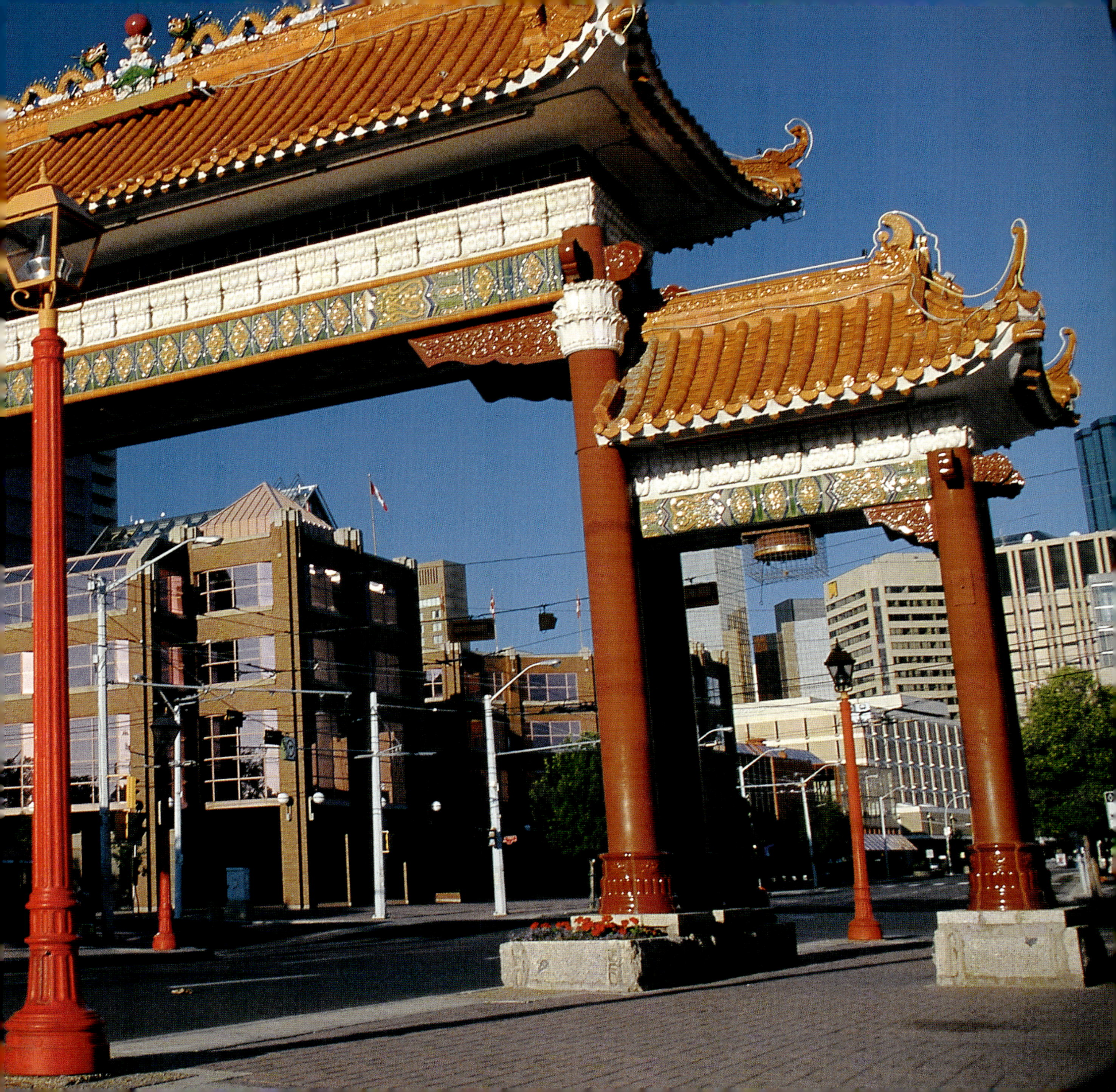

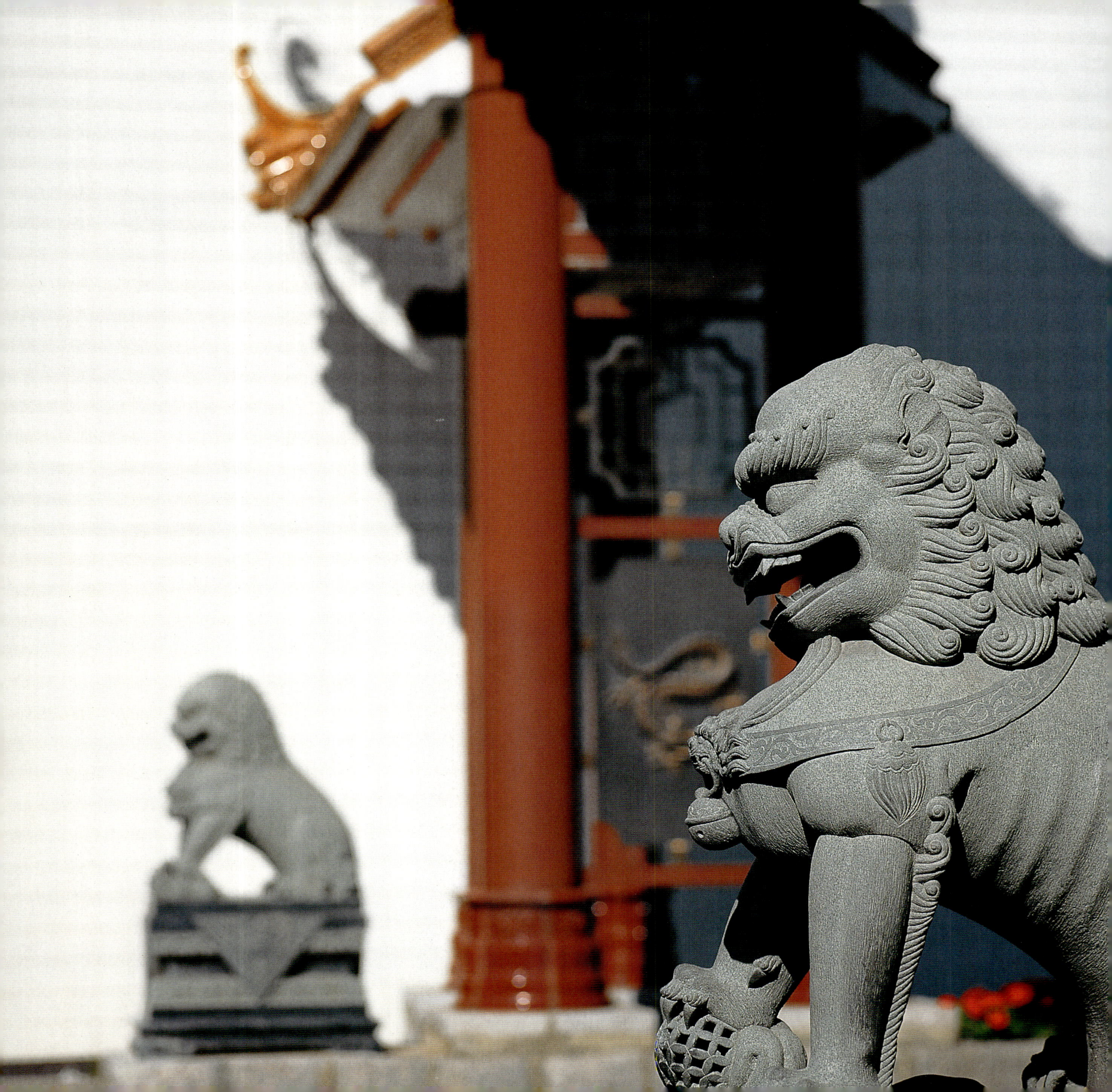

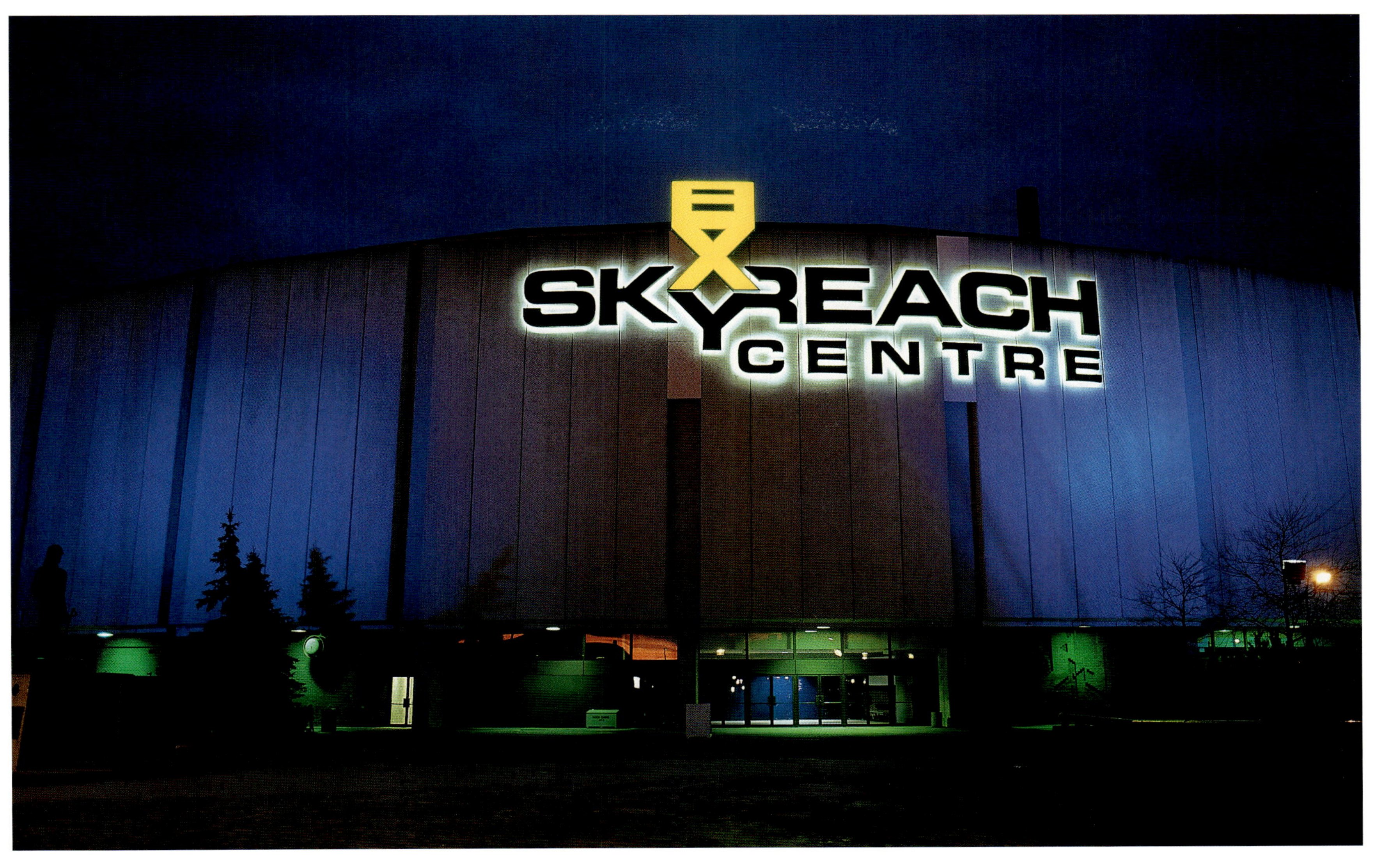

Skyreach Centre is home to the Edmonton Oilers, Wayne Gretzky's first team in the NHL. The Great One set a record for the most goals ever scored in a single season during his time with the Oilers.

These traditional carved lions guard Chinatown Gate. For good luck, many passersby stop to roll the ball in the lion's mouth.

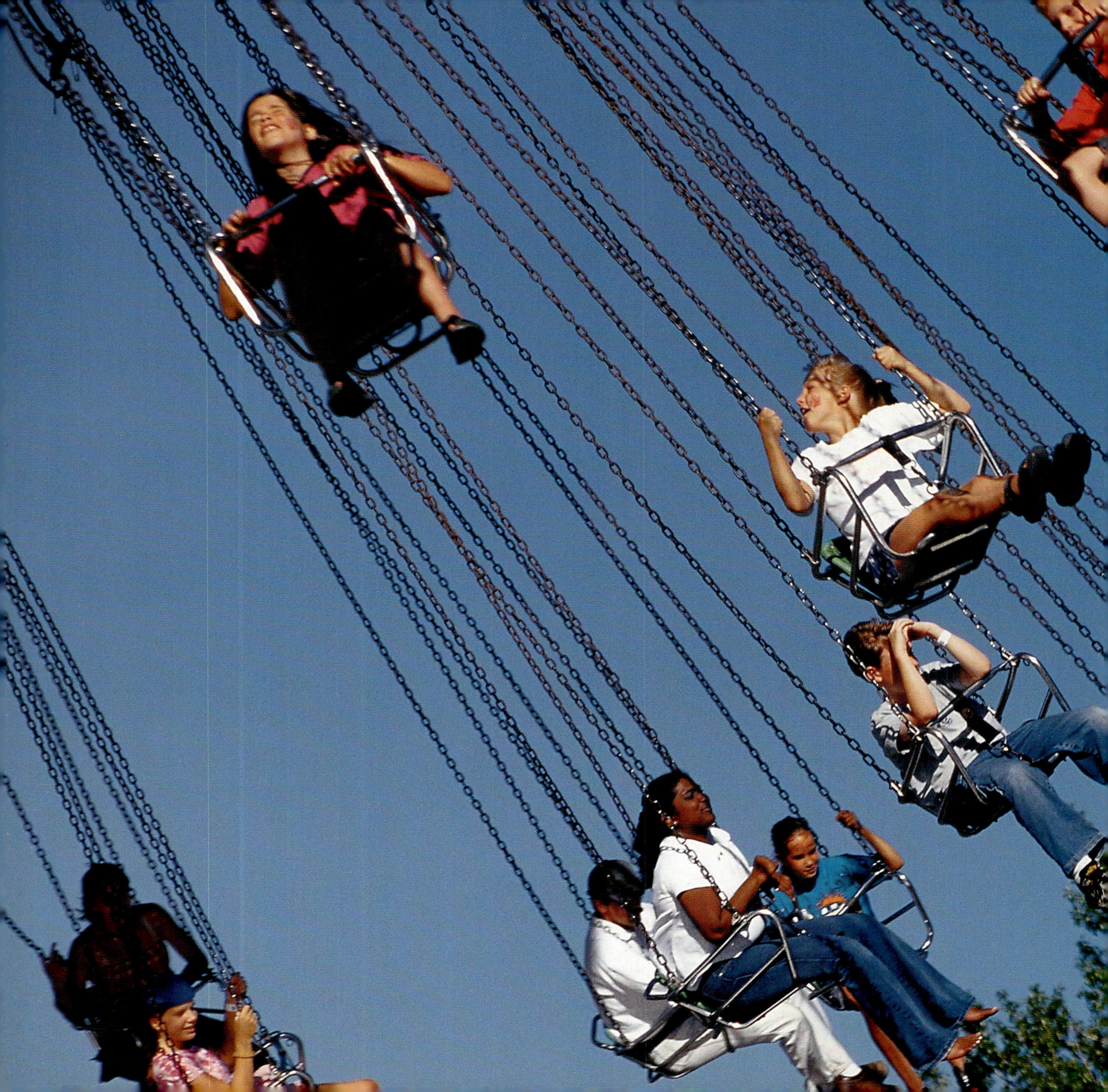

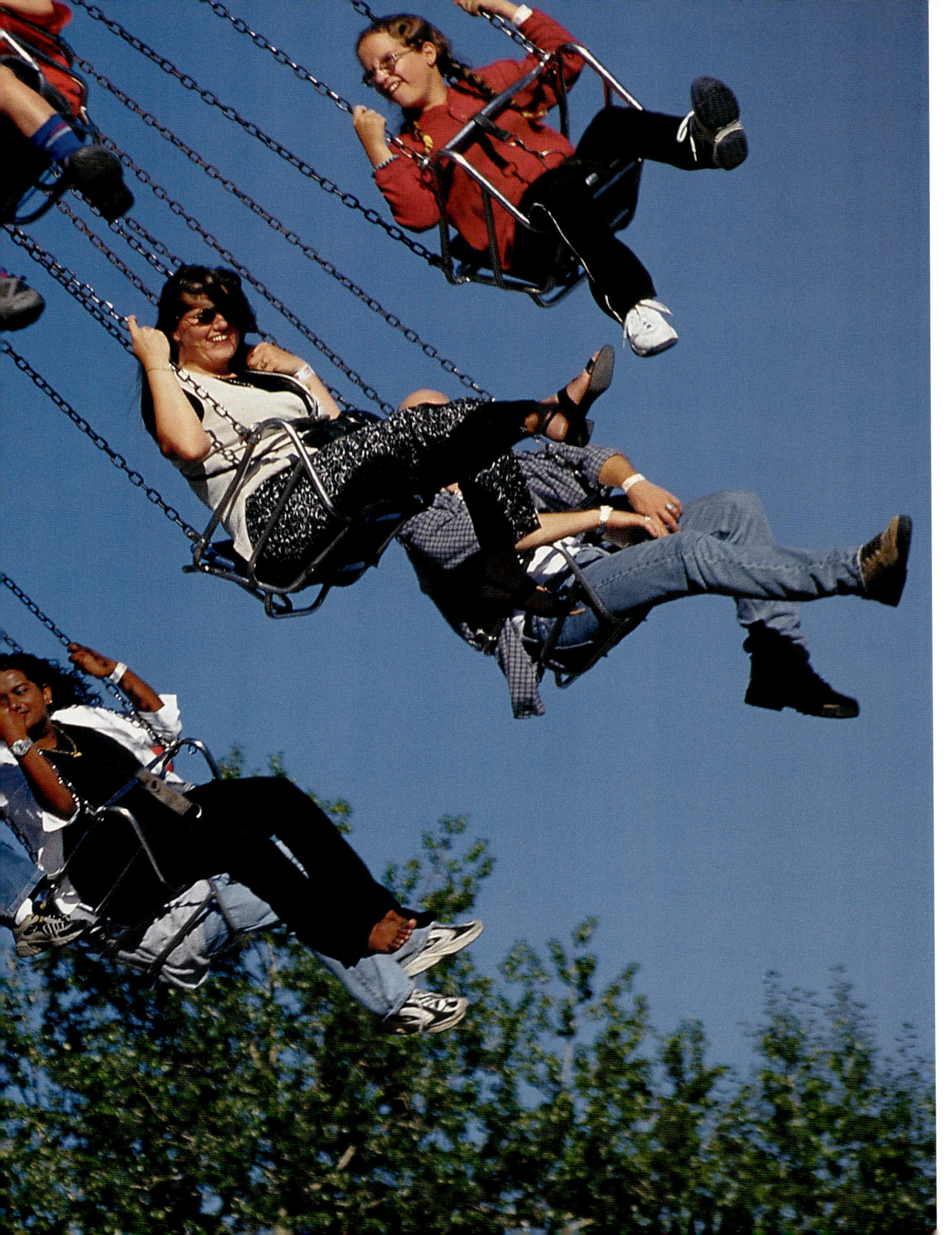

Trapeze acts, parade floats, midway rides, and chuckwagon races — there's so much to see during Edmonton's Klondike Days each July that it's hard to decide where to look. More than 750,000 attend events, from the morning Klondike Breakfasts to the Fun Tubs Derby.

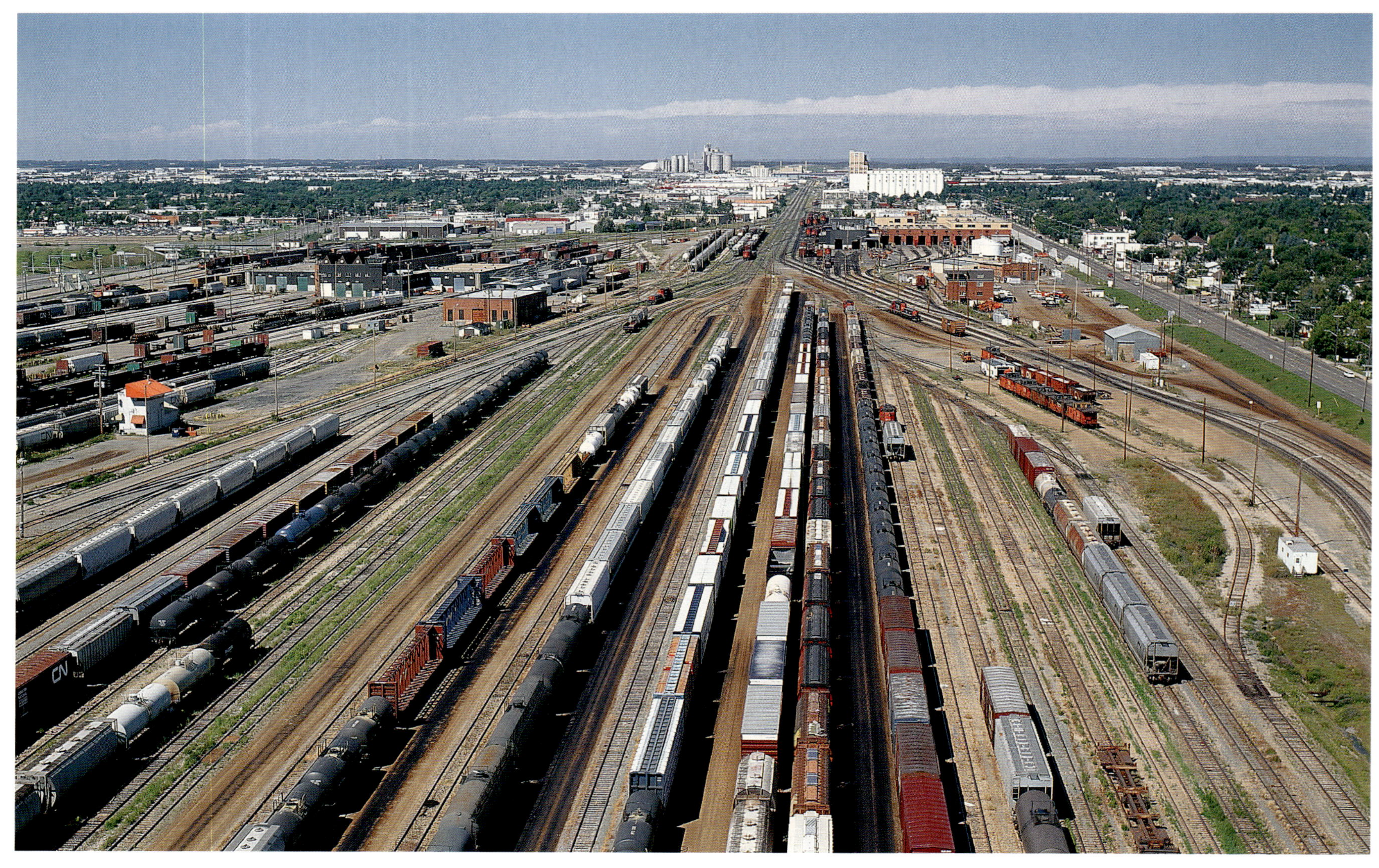

Still integral to Alberta's agriculture industry, rail lines criss-cross the province. At the U.S. border, cargo is shipped through Shelby, Montana. To the west, passengers make their way through B.C. and Jasper National Park towards Edmonton on VIA Rail's luxury cars.

With more than 40 percent of workers boasting post-secondary education, Edmonton has one of Canada's highest numbers of university graduates per capita — part of the reason 900 high-tech companies call this city home.

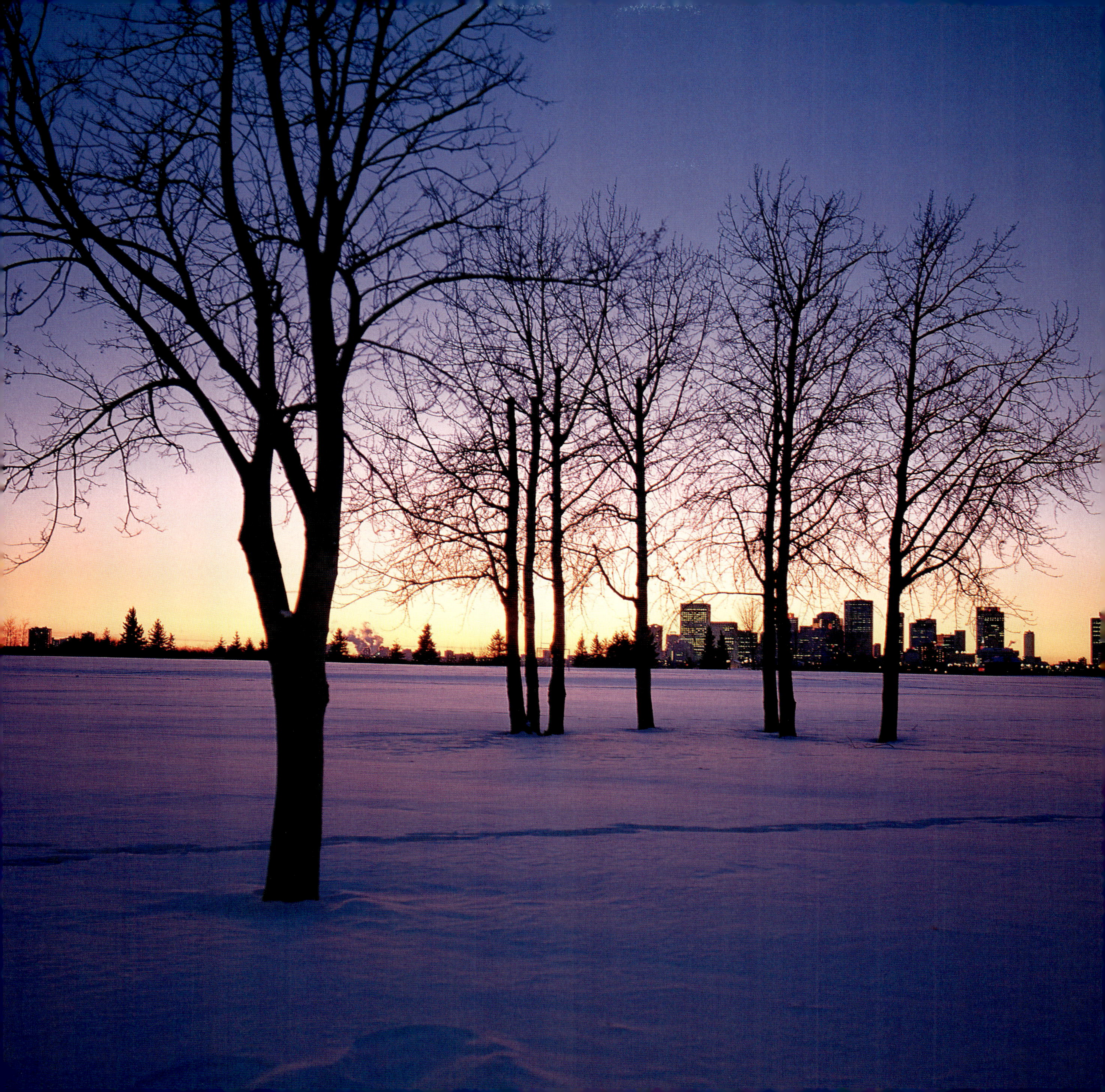

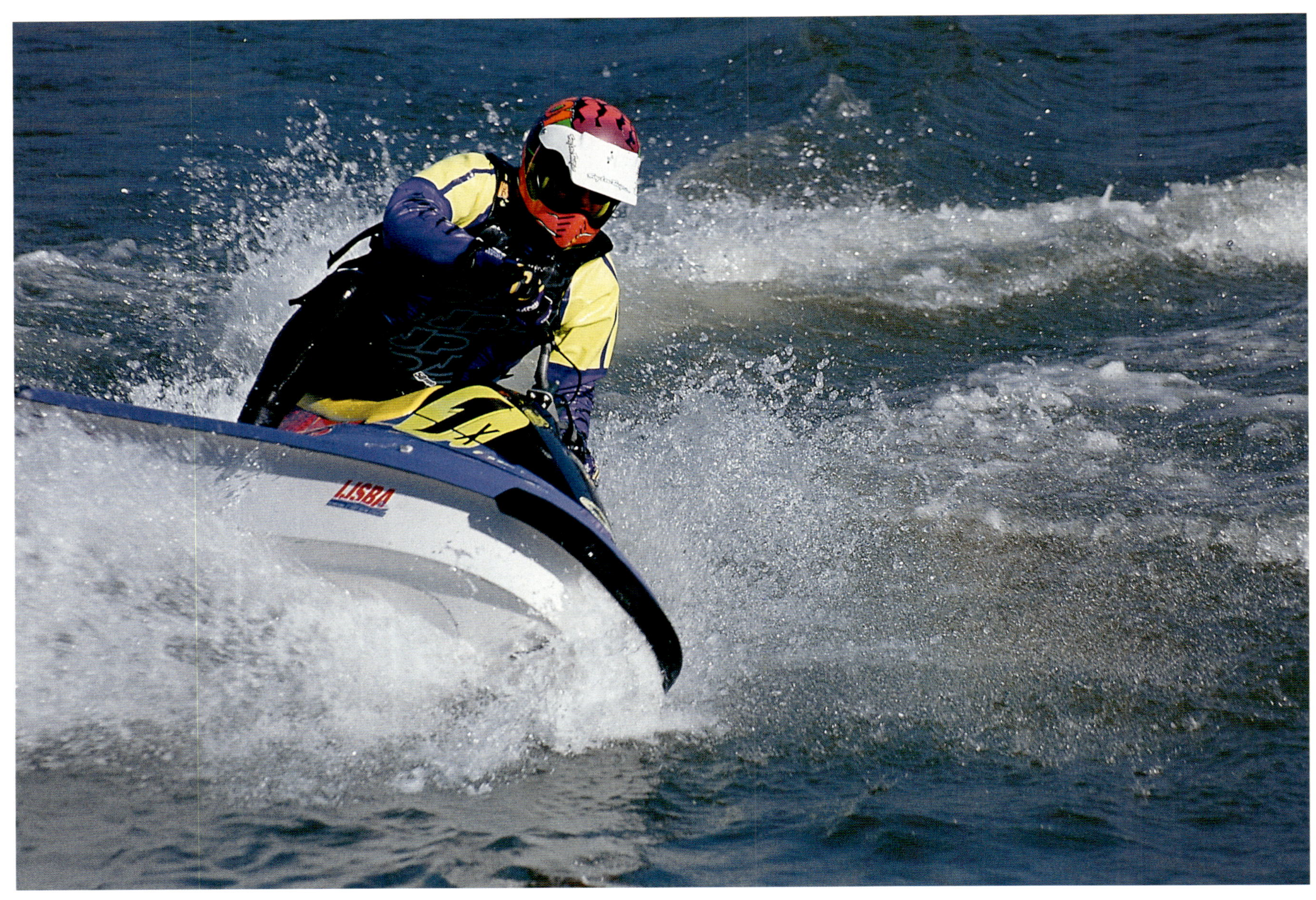

A number of boat launches along the river valley offer access for water sports enthusiasts. Jet skiers, water skiers, and pleasure boaters are a constant sight in the summer months.

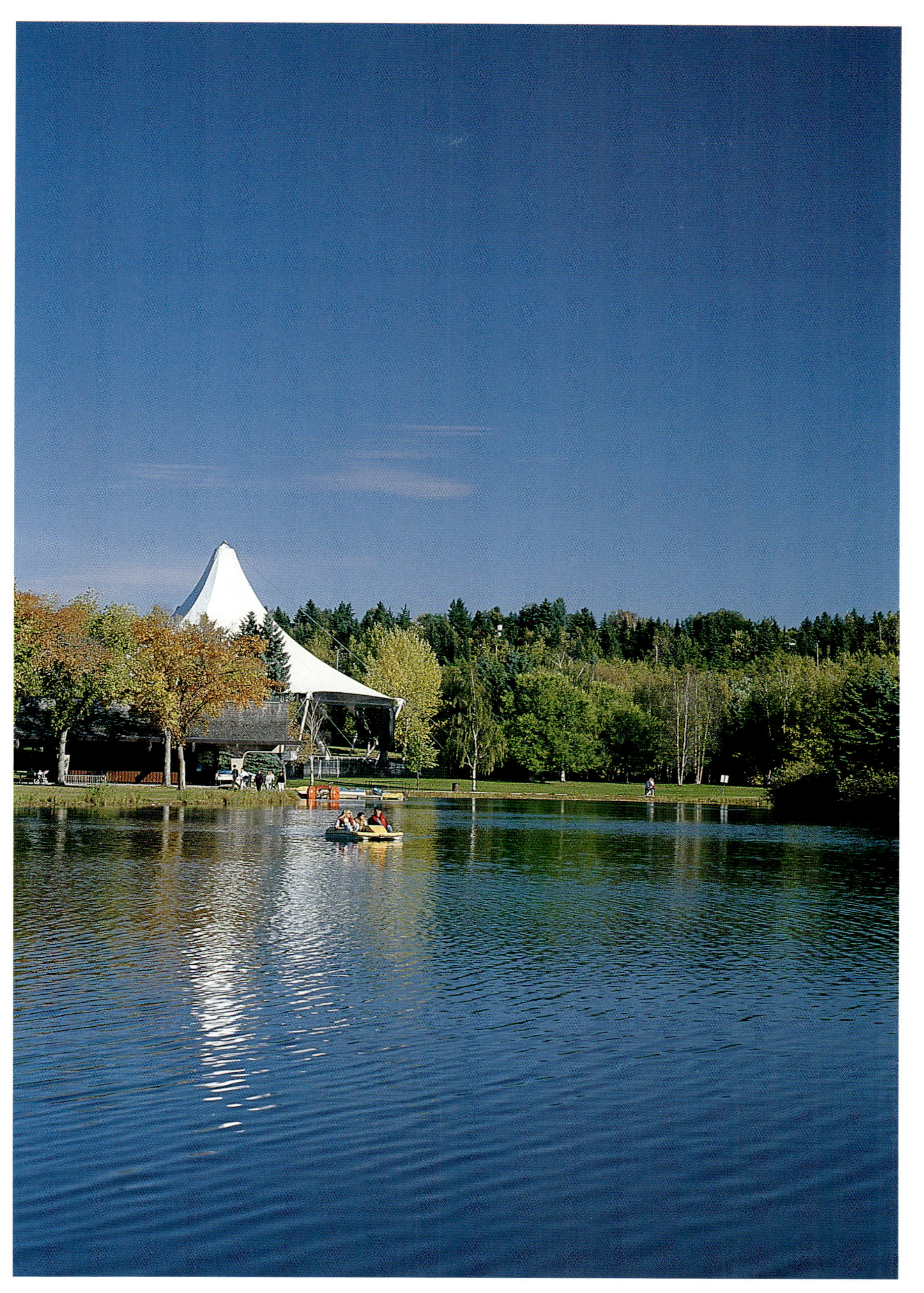

William Hawrelak Park's artificial lake, complete with tranquil shores and beach grasses, is a favourite spot for boaters and bird watchers. In the summer months, the Hawrelak Amphitheatre hosts outdoor festivals and concerts.

Summer's picturesque lake becomes Edmonton's skating pond each winter in William Hawrelak Park. A heated indoor pavilion nearby provides a place to warm up and sip hot chocolate.

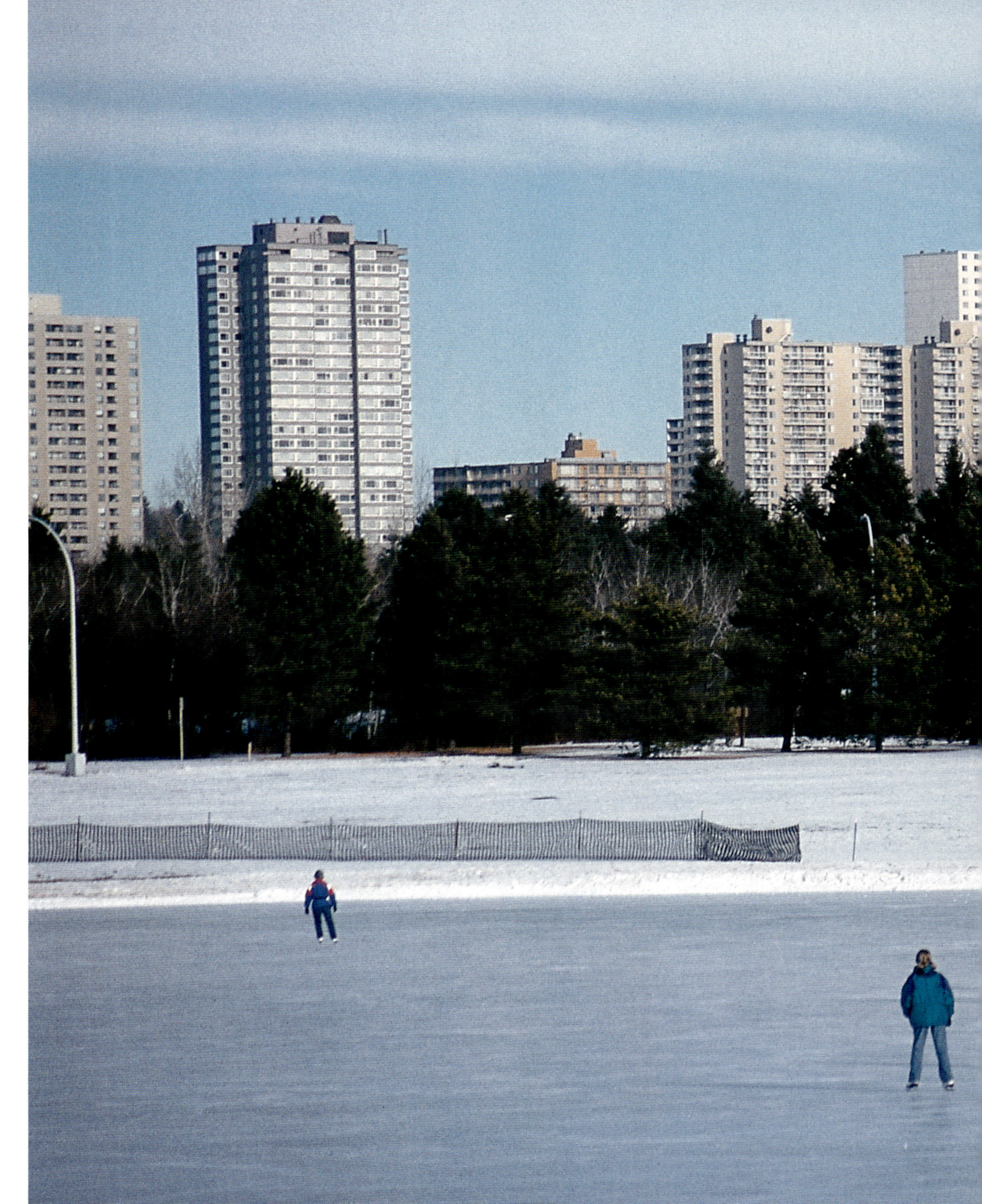

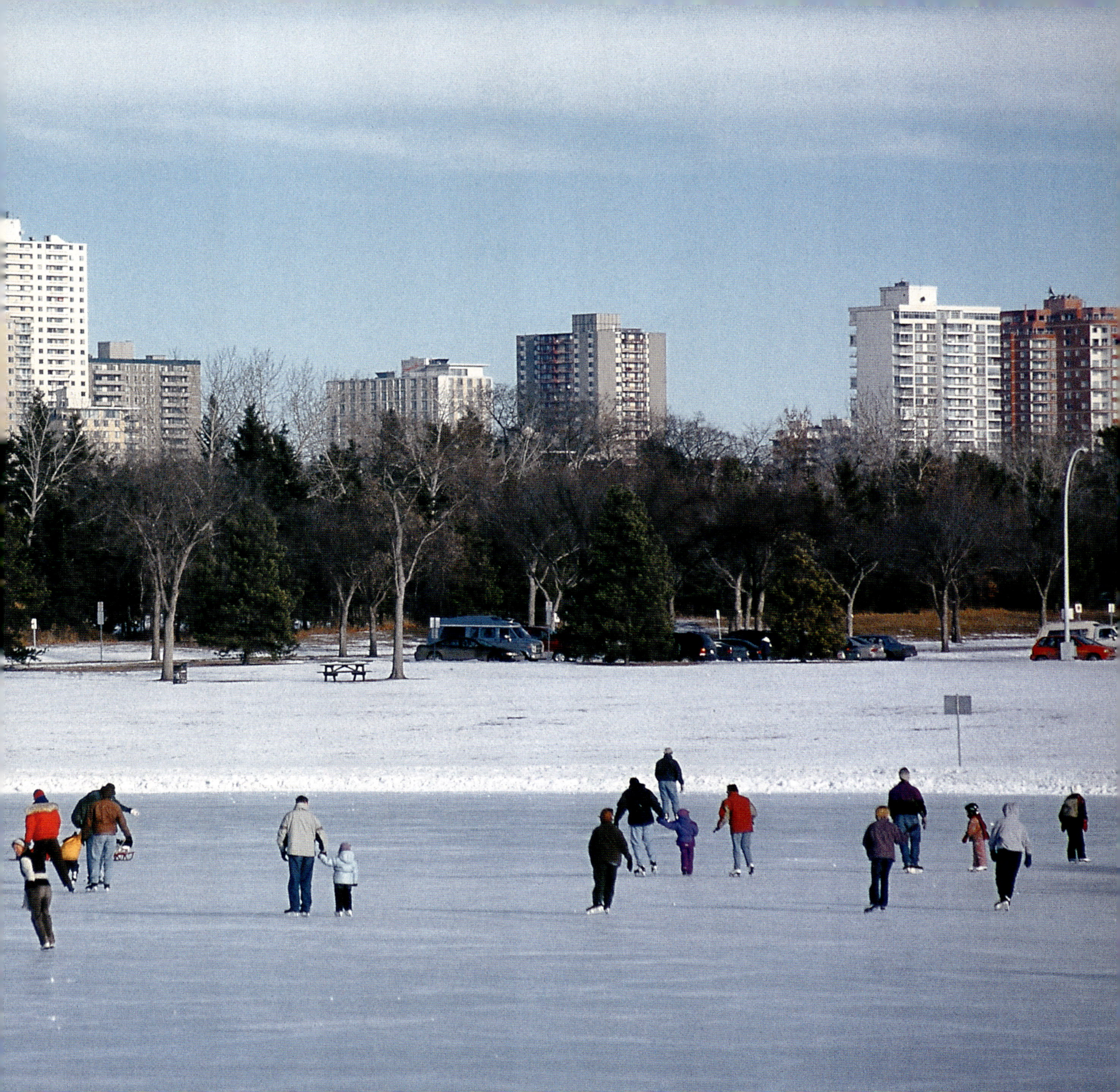

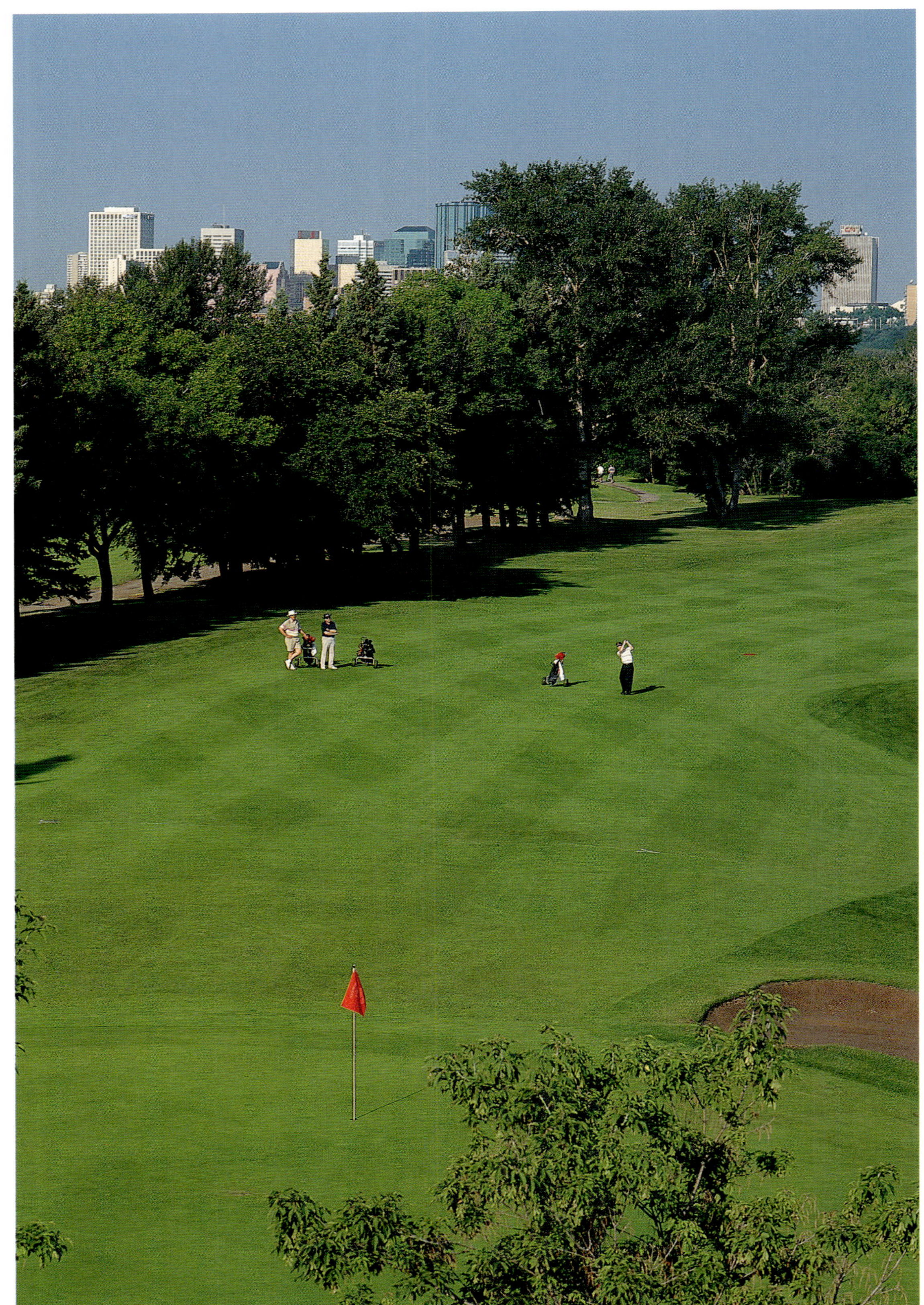

Three public golf courses nestled in the North Saskatchewan River Valley tempt enthusiasts onto the fairways. From the par-three holes of the Rundle Golf Club to the groomed greens of the more challenging Riverside Golf Course, there is something to suit every player.

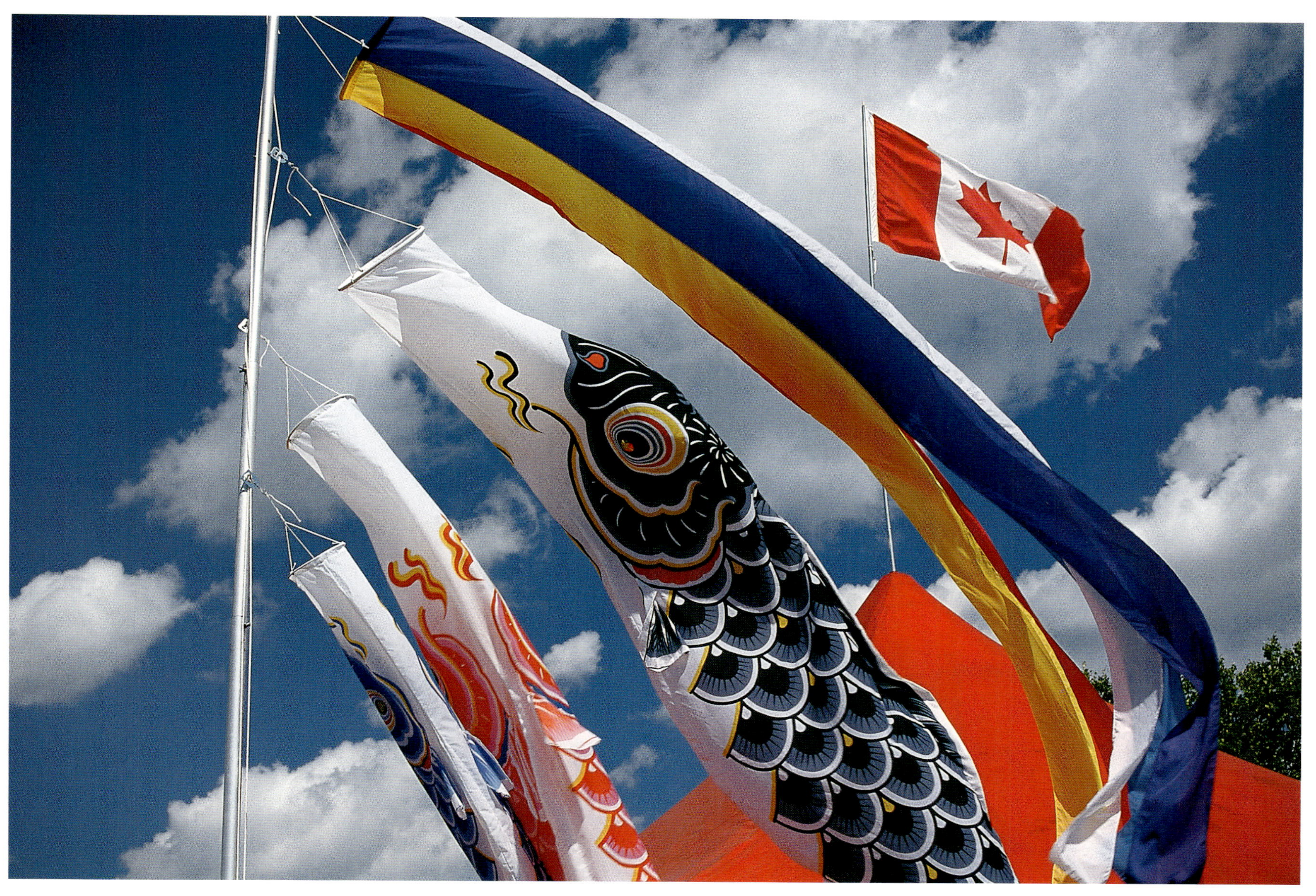

In more than 50 pavilions, performers representing countries from around the world form part of Edmonton's Heritage Days.

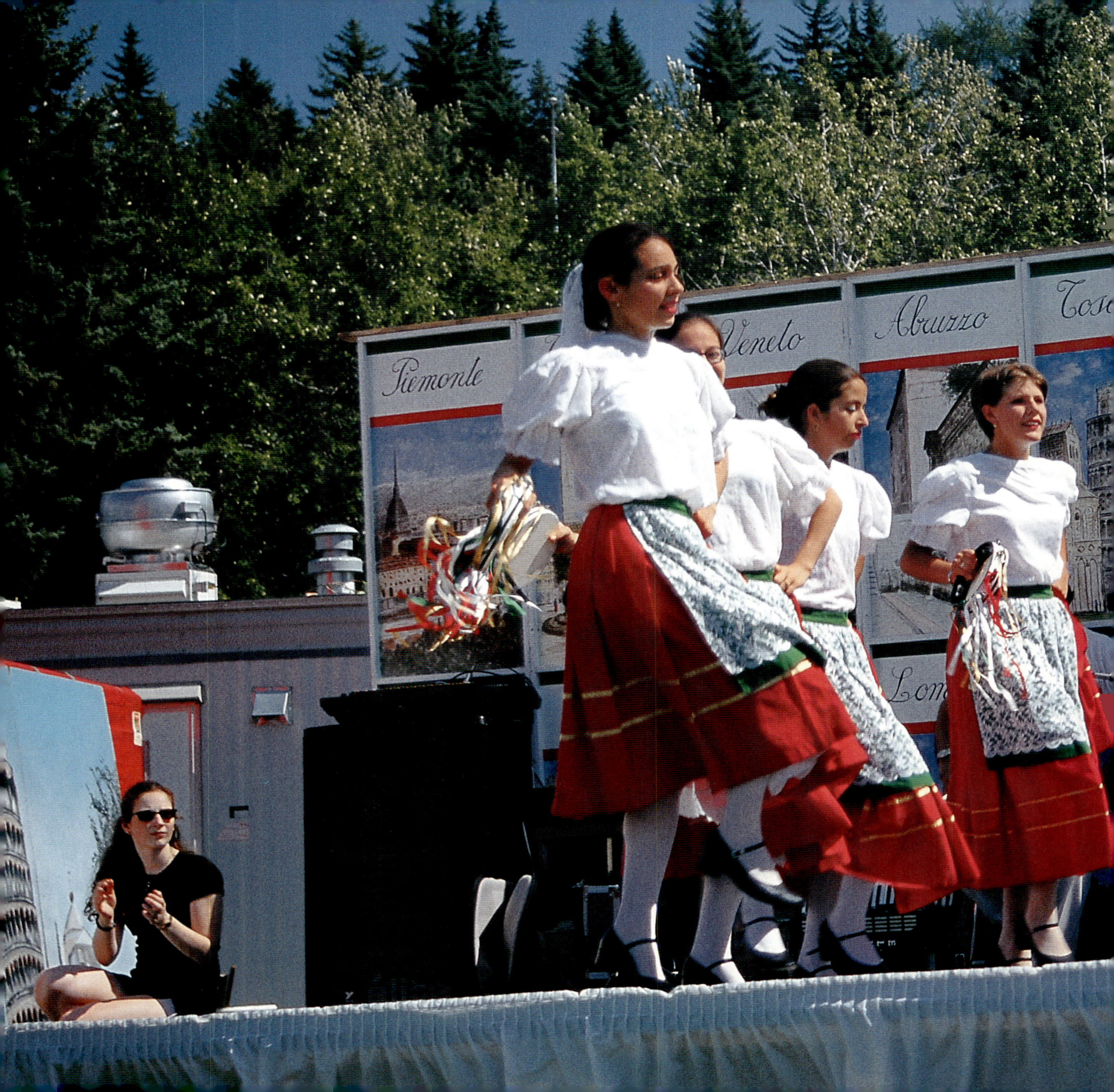
Piemonte
Veneto
Abruzzo

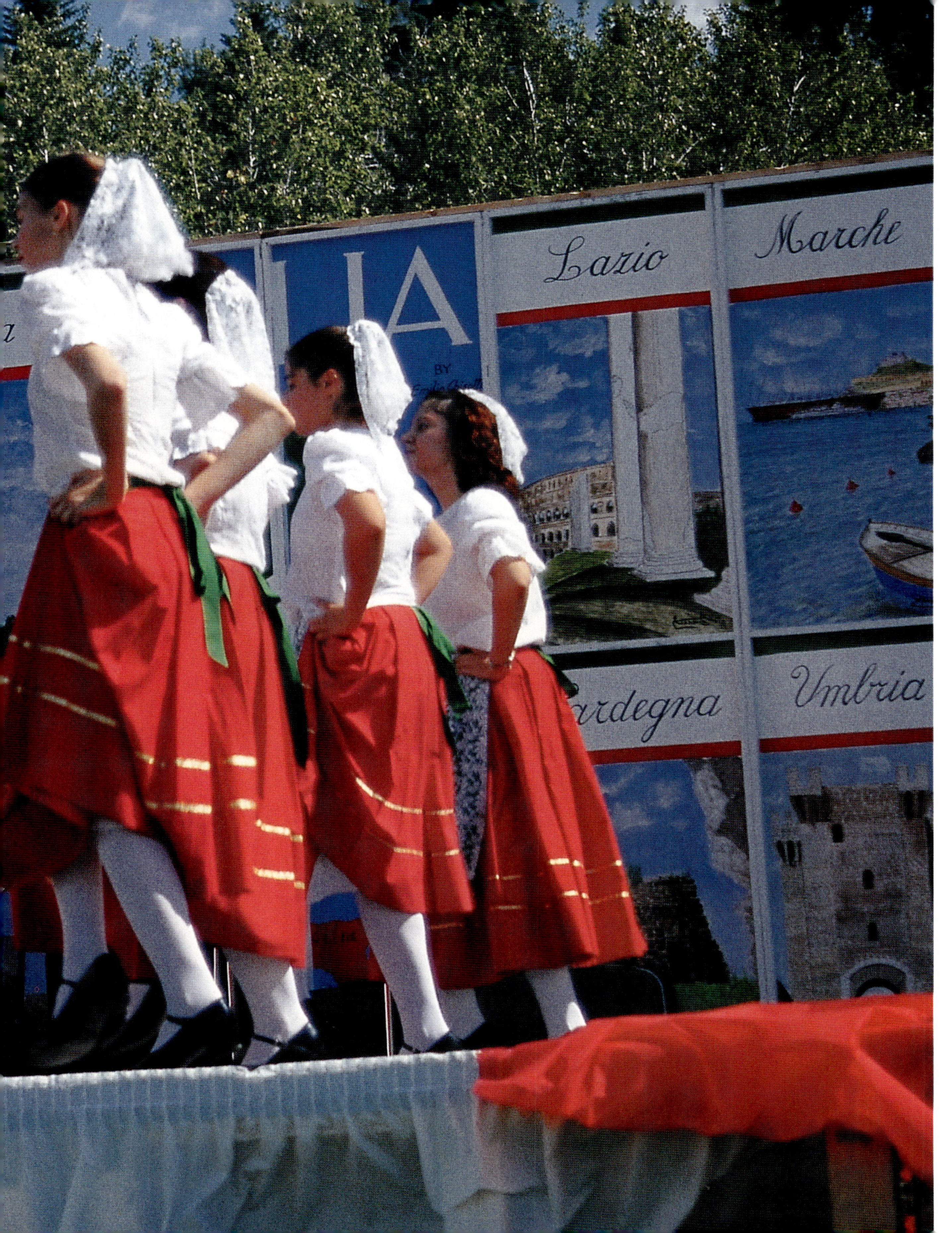

The visitors who flock to William Hawrelak Park for the Heritage Festival find themselves caught up in a whirl of dance and music performances, arts and crafts displays, and more flavours than it would ever be possible to sample during the three-day event.

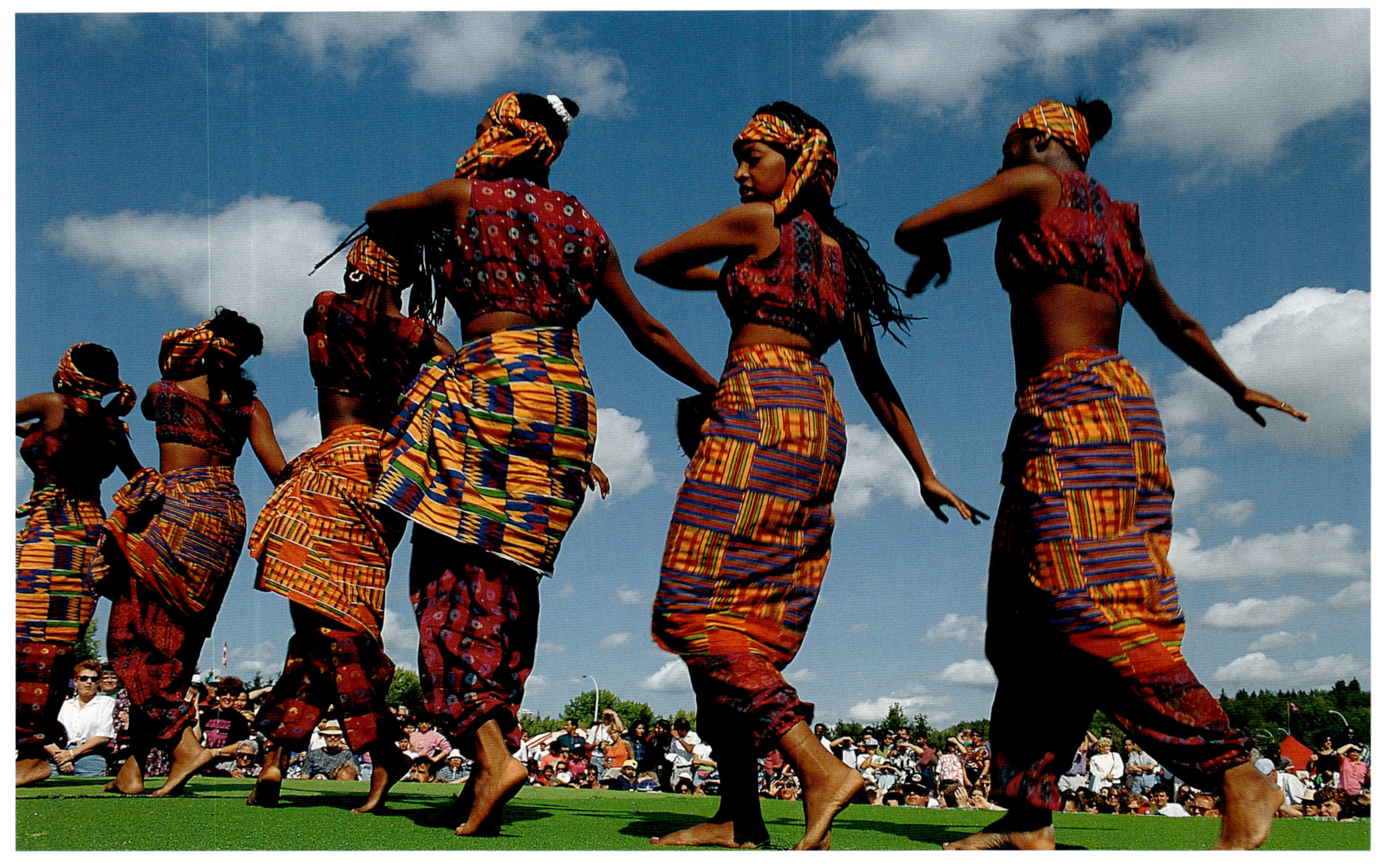

The Heritage Festival is one of 14 major annual events in the city. The new year begins with First Night revelries and continues with the International Street Performers Festival in July, the Folk Music Festival in August, and the Canadian Finals Rodeo in November.

With a 132-kilometre (82-mile) trail network, Edmonton is the perfect place for walking, biking, or in-line skating. The city also offers nature-lovers the choice of 22 parks, 11 lakes, and 14 ravines.

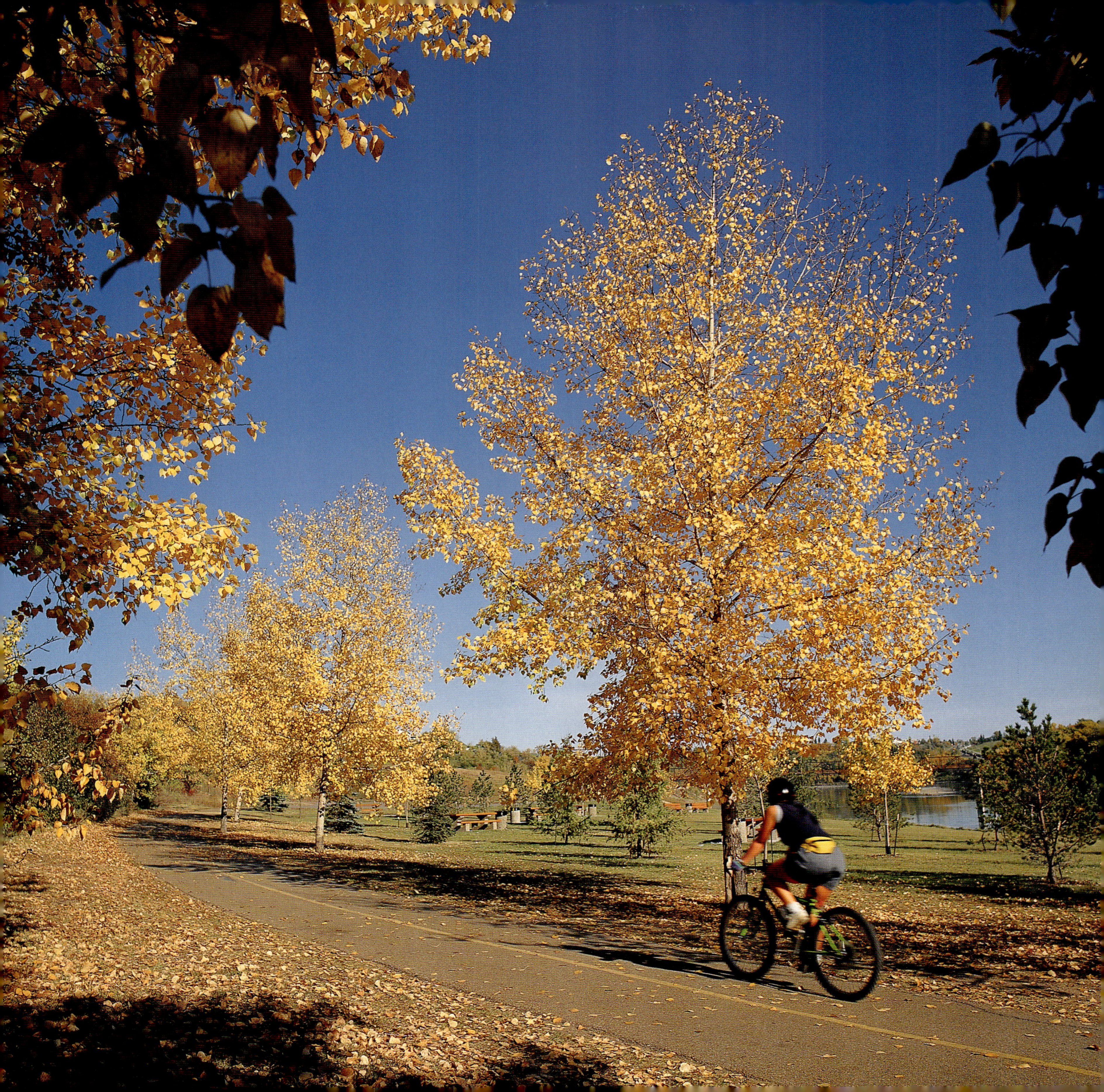

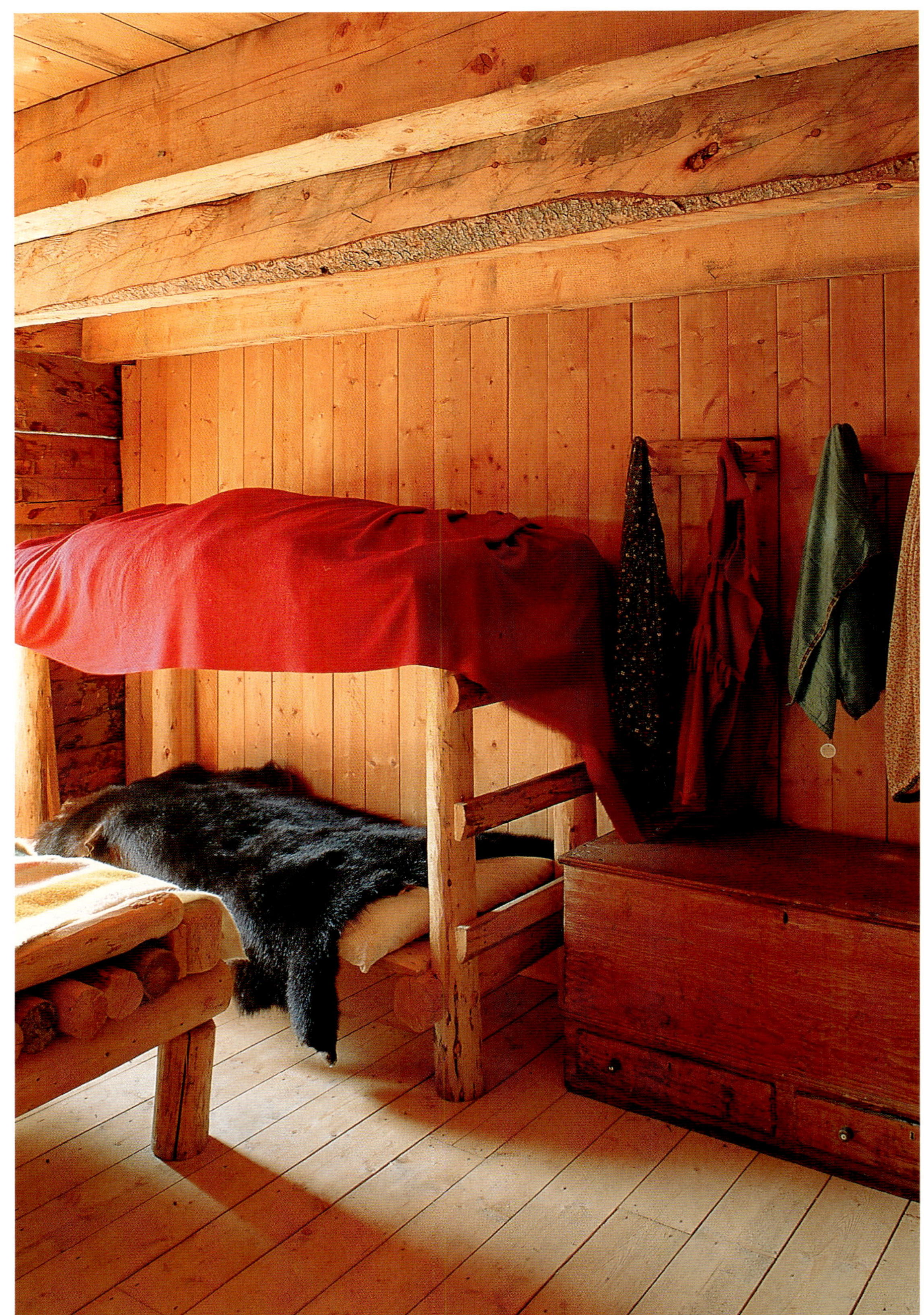

The Hudson's Bay Company established its first fort in the area in 1795 and christened it Edmonton House, after the English home town of Chief Factor Tomlinson. Ten years after the Hudson's Bay Company merged with its rival, the North West Company, in 1821, a new fort was created — Fort Edmonton.

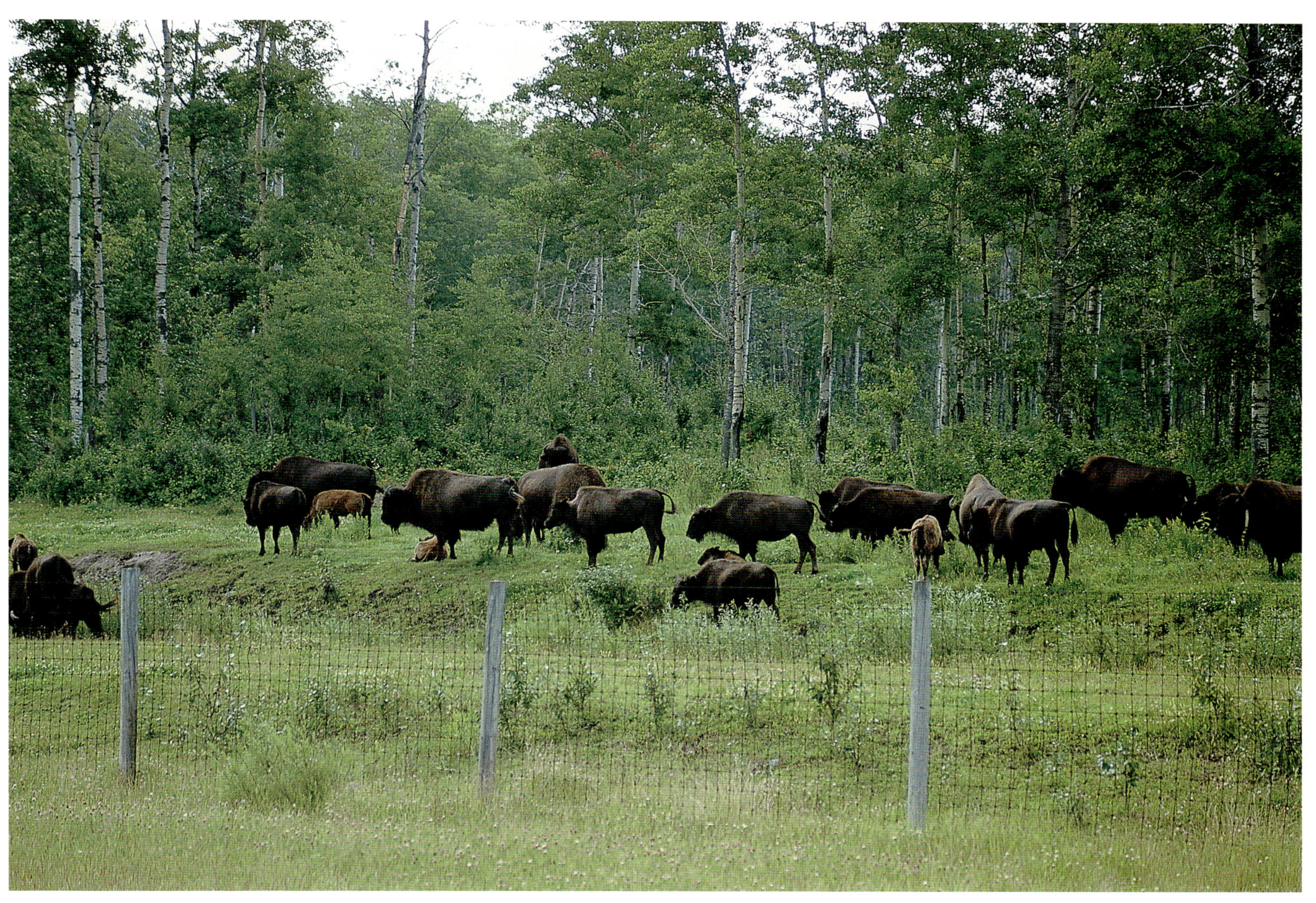

In the early 1900s, Elk Island National Park was the site of a massive and successful attempt to rebuild the area's once-thriving population of large mammals. More than 750 plains bison, 335 wood bison, and 1,700 elk now roam the reserve, a half-hour drive east of Edmonton.

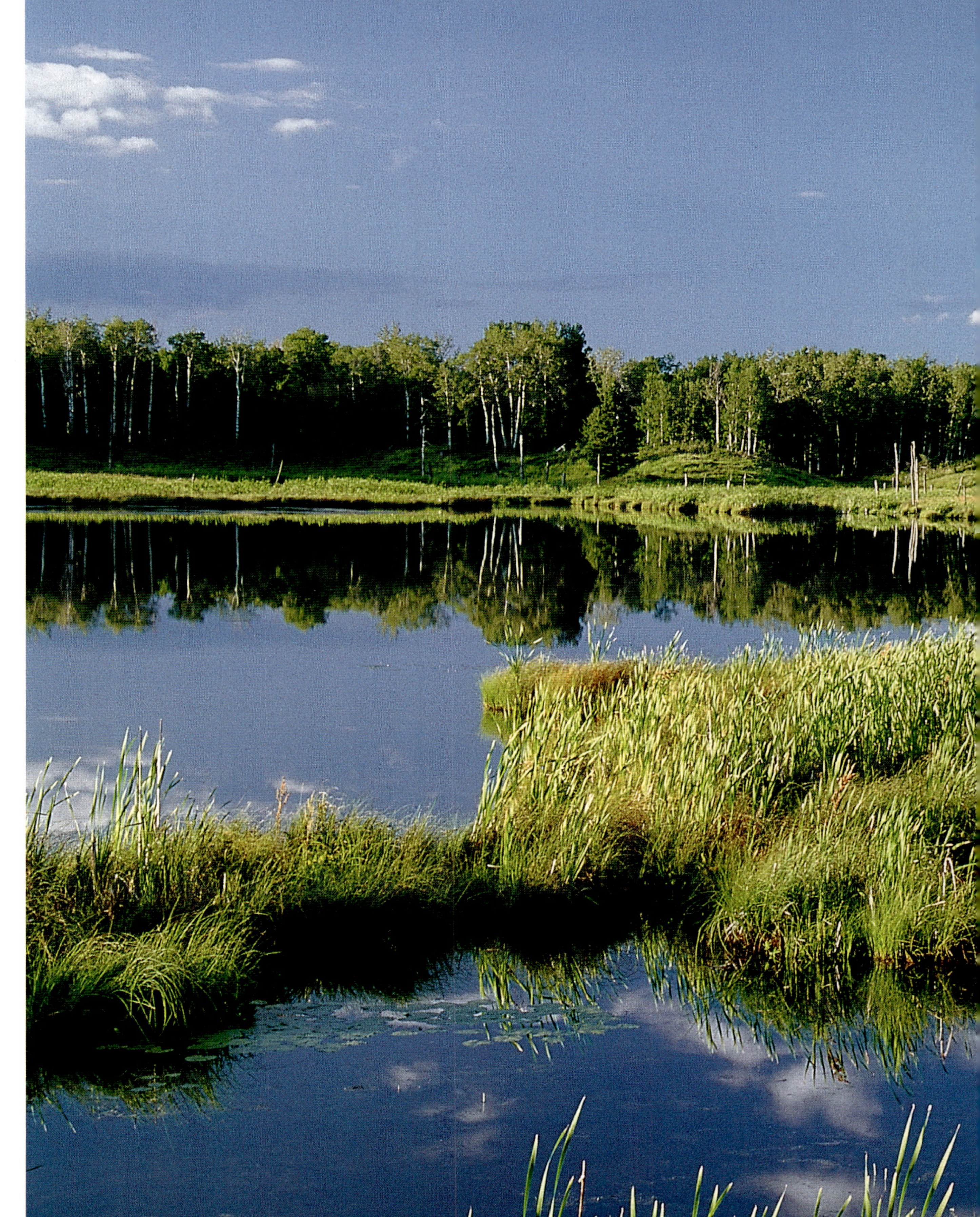

Eleven trails in Elk Island National Park lead through secluded meadows and aspen groves, allowing hikers to watch for the park's reclusive wildlife.

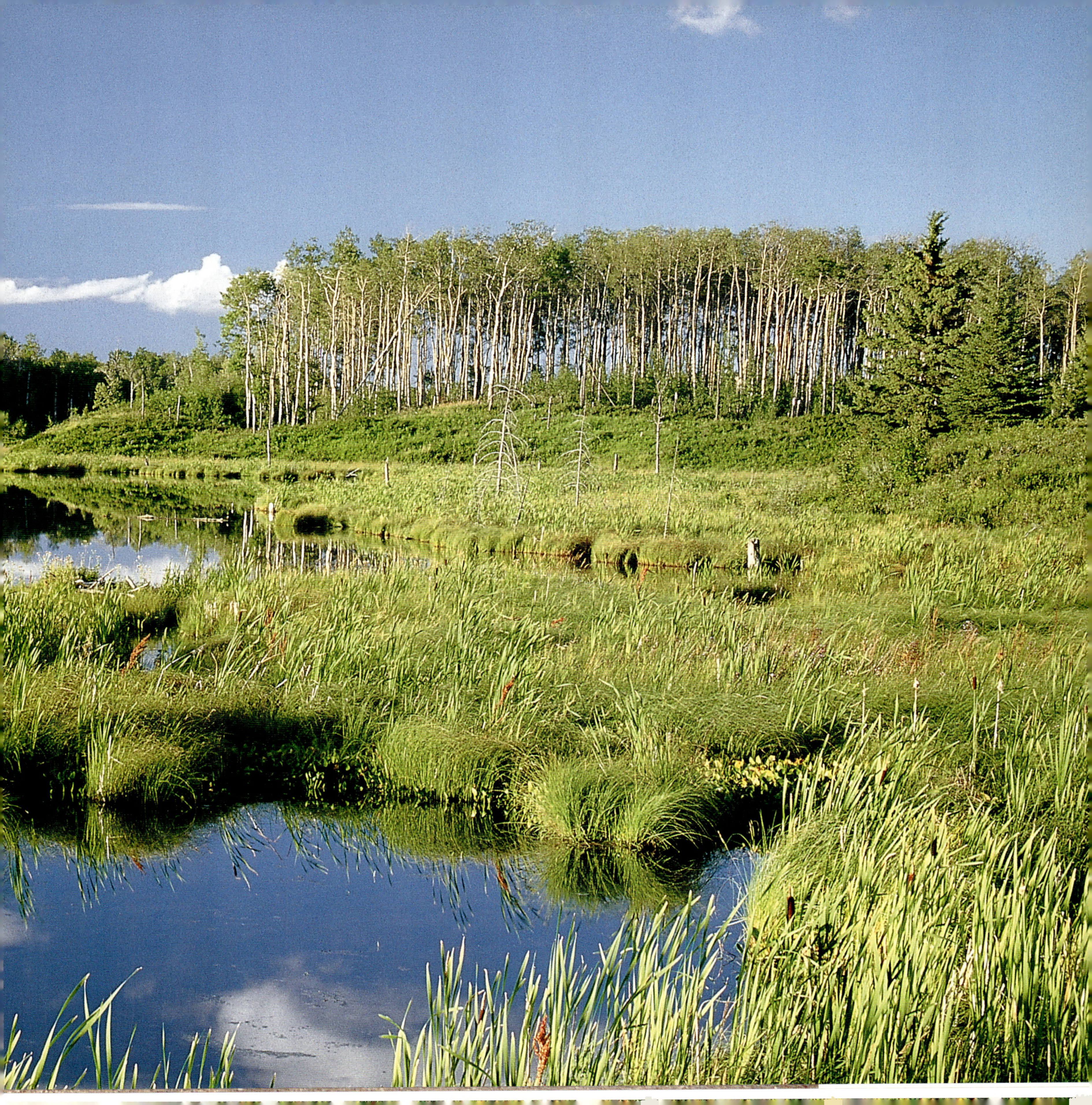

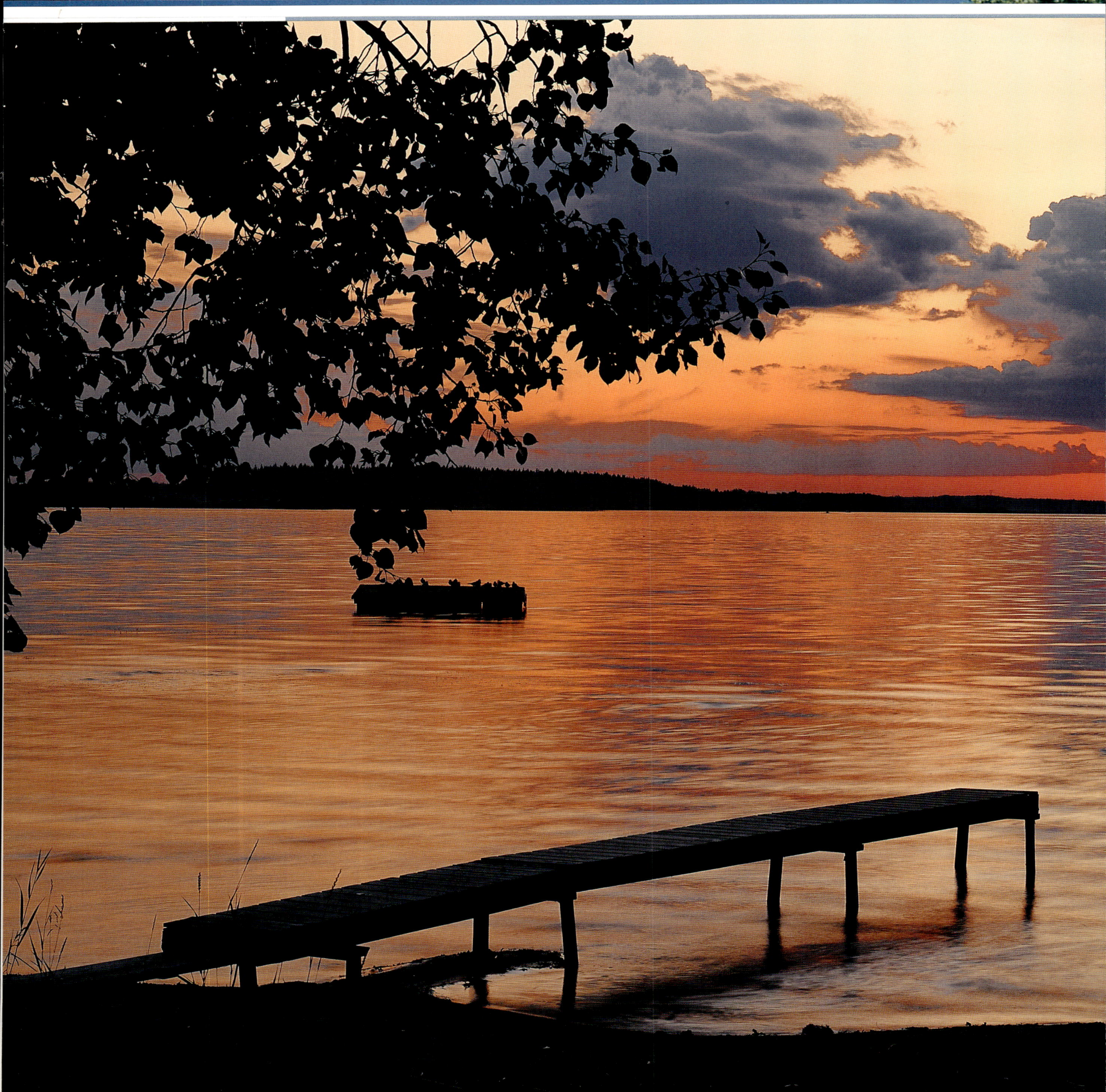

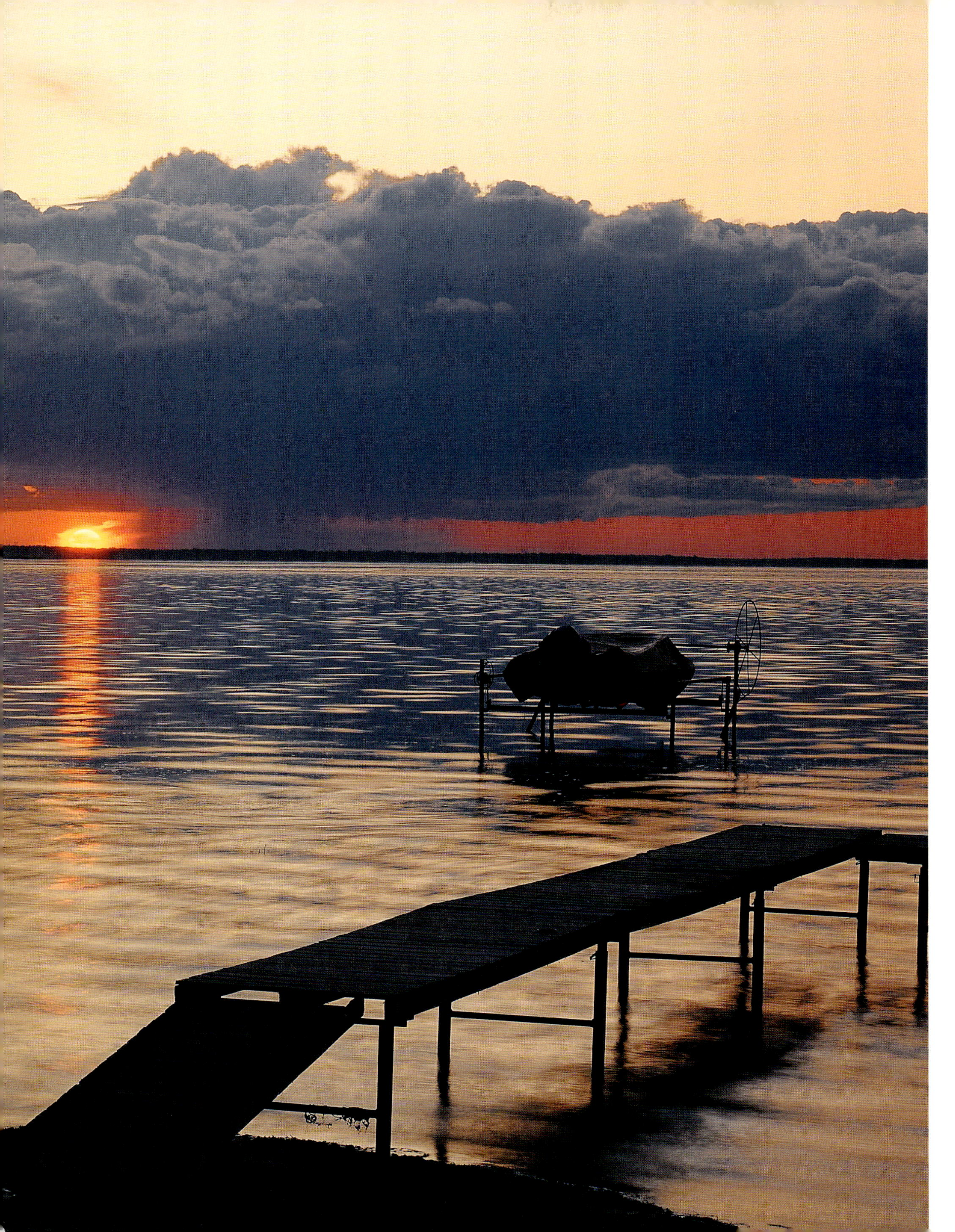

Edmonton residents looking for a summer escape find it on the shores of Lac Ste. Anne, just west of the city. Walleye, perch, and whitefish attract anglers, while others come to waterski, sail, and windsurf.

Photo Credits

THE KELLY GROUP/MACH 2 STOCK 1, 3, 10-11, 16-17, 20, 24, 25, 31, 48, 49, 52, 53, 56-57, 62, 63, 65, 68, 70-71, 72, 73, 78, 83

LESLIE DEGNER 6-7, 8, 9, 14, 15, 18, 19, 21, 22-23, 26, 27, 32, 34, 35, 42-43, 46-47, 58, 59, 60-61, 64, 75

MARIE SEDIVY 12

WAYNE LYNCH 13

TROY & MARY PARLEE 28-29, 30, 36-37, 54-55

DUANE S. RADFORD/LONE PINE PHOTO 33, 38, 40, 44, 45, 66-67, 79, 80-81, 88-89

JAMES BURTON/MACH 2 STOCK 39, 94-95

MARK DEGNER 41, 69, 76-77

TONY MAXWELL/MACH 2 STOCK 50-51

CLARENE W. NORRIS/LONE PINE PHOTO 74, 90, 91

DAVID SCHAEFER/MACH 2 STOCK 82, 84, 92-93

WAYNE SHIELS/LONE PINE PHOTO 85, 86-87